Pray Your Way Out:

The Journey To Escape

Antaneeca Simmons
5-25-2018

Acknowledgment

Pray Your Way Out
Copyright © 2018 by Antaneeca Simmons
Published by Antaneeca Simmons
Birmingham, AL.

Cover design: fiverr.com/Laruia
Editor: Molly Erickson
Editor: Carol Colson
First Printing 2018
Printed in the United States of America

Scripture references are from The Holy Bible.
All rights reserved.
ISBN- 13: 978-1720309079
ISBN- 10:1720309078

Contents

Dedication

This book is dedicated to those who have survived, are currently victims, and the innocent lives lost to domestic violence. A special thank you to Nichole Freemen, Tonya Baker, Kimberly Clark, Jolie Halsey, Bernadette Edwards, Winne Lowe-Davis, Lucinda Moore, Latina Rueben, Lauren Smith, Ashely Moore, Keyana Lewis, Candace Brown, Allison Dearing, Beverly McClendon and my mother Mildred Bearden for helping me escape. To my husband Larry Simmons and our three boys, thank you for your unconditional love and support and most of all my heavenly Father for his grace and mercy.

Introduction

"Now I lay me down to sleep I pray the Lord my soul to keep. If I shall die before I wake I pray the Lord my soul to take"

Abuse. It can happen to anyone at any time. Every 15 seconds a woman is abused in the U.S. It does not discriminate against age, race, gender, or financial status. Every 1 and 3 American women will be the victim of abuse at least once in their lifetime. When leaving, victims ask the question "Lord, why me?" At least I did.

I must have prayed this prayer a thousand times. Trying to understand abuse should be easy but it's not. It's difficult and dangerous and confusing. How can a person who says they love you bring harm to your mind, body, and soul? Life is already a puzzle of 1000 different pieces and abuse makes you feel like the pieces will never fit. So many nights I cried with guilt and shame. Some nights however I fought! I fought with every inch of my being against the depression and guilt and shame. I must have had three different personalities trying to compete: Love, Hope, and Defeat.

Somehow abuse leaves you as the victim trapped in between

love and hate. Mostly self-hate. How do you fix self-hate?

How do you feel worthy again? How do you forgive? How

do you escape? How do you pick up the broken pieces and

start over? You pray your way out.

Pray without ceasing 1 Thessalonians 5:17

Chapter One

"And fear not them which kill the body but are not able to kill the soul: but rather fear him which is able to and destroy both soul body in hell." Matthew 10:29

It was a beautiful midsummer morning. In Mississippi, every sunset seemed to be beautiful. Ruby lived in a small town called Lakeside on the gulf coast. To the south of her was beautiful sandy beaches and to the north of her were mountains. Beautiful mountains in the distance. On any given morning you could see the sunset dancing off the ocean or peeking through the mountains and trees. The population was only 2500 people, so everyone was like neighbors.

Ruby's family was well known in the town. They lived in the biggest house in their little village, as some would call it. It was a three-story white house about 3,200 square feet. Everyone raved about the landscape and people would often drive from miles away to see it. Her stepfather Willie had a green thumb. On the porch stood two tall trees, one on each

A. Simmons

side of the door. The front of the house was covered with pink and white roses on each side. There was also a pond in the front of the house with a fountain in the middle. On both sides of the pond stood two beautiful cherry blossom trees that hung perfectly over a swing bench. There was a little walking trail from the front to the back leading to the pool and the pool house. Ruby had tried to incorporate every element that brought her peace right in her own yard.

Chapter Two

Ruby was a model and actress. She stood 5'9" and weighed 125. She was a beautiful dark skinned African-American woman with long curly black hair. Her career had bought her enough wealth to take care of her parents, so she built a home big enough for her parents and her 9yr old son Henry. Ruby adored her mother, Mrs. Lily Smith. She was a cancer survivor, retired teacher, and a true missionary in her right, selflessly serving others. If you ever asked about "Mrs. Sweet Lily," people always said the same thing. "I've never met anybody as giving and sweet." Ruby followed in her mom's footsteps. She had started a foundation for the homeless in her community. Ruby seemed to have it all. She loved the Lord, had an amazing son, a close relationship with her mom, and successful career. There was only one problem. For the past 3yrs Ruby had been in an abusive relationship with her on-again-off-again fiancé Luke Johnson, also known as Mr. Charismatic.

A. Simmons

Of course, Luke didn't start off abusive. They'd meet at a local jazz spot in Lakeside. Ruby had never seen him before. He used his charm to win her over that night. There new friendship quickly blossomed into something more. Ruby had been in very high-profile relationship working as a model and wanted something a little more normal. Luke was able to give her that. He started off as the perfect gentlemen but the closer they got, his gentlemanly mannerism turned in to paranoia and control.

Luke was new to the Lakeside community. He'd only been there for as long as he and Ruby had been dating. He was extra nice to the elderly ladies in the neighborhood, which is how he got the name Mr. Charismatic, and could talk sports with just about anyone. He was a tall dark athletic African-American man who won people over with his charm and smile. However, he was also a perfect example of a narcissist. A narcissist is someone who has an excessive interest in or admiration of themselves. They are usually arrogant, manipulative, refuse to take the blame for their actions, and profess to be some type of supreme being. He also suffered from bipolar disorder and was extremely abusive, both mentally and physically. Ruth had left several times but always seemed to go back. This morning was different. It was the day she'd decided to walk away but first, she had to get away.

Chapter Three

The night before, Luke shown up at Ruby's house unannounced. It was about two in the morning when the doorbell rang. Ruby knew it had to be him. Mark 3:27 quickly jumped into her spirit. "No man can enter into a strong man's house, and spoil his goods, except he will first bind the strong man; and then he will spoil his house." Ruby knew she was letting the devil himself in. With her hand on the doorknob, Ruby hesitantly said to God "I know he shouldn't come in, but I don't want to wake my mom, stepdad, and Henry, Father," so she opened the door and quickly let him in. Luke was extremely drunk and stumbled to Ruby's room.

By this time the people of Lakeside had caught on to his little secrets. He was becoming the unemployed, abusive neighborhood drunk. Her mom despised their relationship and had been pleading with her to leave. As they both lay in bed, Ruby flat on her back, fully dressed, wrapped in a separate blanket and Luke on top of the covers with nothing but his underwear, Ruby began to pray.

> *"Now I lay me down to sleep, I pray the Lord my soul to keep, if I shall die before I wake, I pray the Lord my soul to take. Father, I'm sorry for staying as long as I have but if you just help me make it through the night I promise I won't go back this time."*

Of course, Luke tried to touch Ruby, but she softly replied: "Please don't touch me, Luke." Surprisingly it worked. Ruby dozed off and before she knew it, it was 6 a.m. "Luke, Luke," Ruby said as she tried to wake him up. "Get up Luke, I'm taking you where you need to go," Ruby said. Still reeking with alcohol Luke rolled over on his other side and ignored Ruby. "Luke," said Ruby "Get up it's time to go now." This time Luke got up angry and quiet.

Ruby rushed him along trying to make it out of the house before her mother or son got up. She opened the door and checked her son's room before bringing Luke out. The coast was clear, so Ruby waved her hand at Luke to come out the room. Ruby prayed everything would go smoothly in the car ride over and it seemed to be until they got to the freeway.

Upon getting in the car Ruby asked, "Where would you like to go?"

Luke replied, "The Shop." The Shop was located about 20 minutes from Lakeside in Cedarbrook. It was one of the local barbershops. It was a brick building with glass windows across the front, a few sofas for seating and about 3 barber chairs. Mr. Bailey was the owner and would let Luke sleep there from time to time since he didn't have any place else to go. Ruby thought nothing of it and jumped on the freeway.

Luke finally begin to talk. "You think you're just going to leave me," He said. Ruby didn't say a word. He said it again, "You think you're just going to leave me?" Luke said but this time he was furious and begin to beat Ruby in the head. Ruby still didn't say a word. Luke continued to strike Ruby in her head over and over. Ruby was terrified of running off the road, so she held tight to the steering wheel and kept on driving. The twenty-minute drive seemed like an eternity. The freeway was empty. It was an early Saturday morning so any hope of a passerby noticing the abuse was slim to none. Luke continued to beat her in the head screaming "You think you just going to leave me like this," "You're a worthless piece of shit," "Where is your God now." Ruby wanted to scream or jump out of the car, but she knew she couldn't. With tears rolling down her face she began to say Psalm 23 to herself:

> "The LORD is my shepherd; I shall not want. He maketh me to lie down in green pastures: he leadeth me beside the still waters, He restoreth my soul: he leadeth me in the paths of righteousness for his name's sake. Yea, though I walk through the valley of the shadow of death, I will fear no evil: for thou art with me; thy rod and thy staff they comfort me. Thou preparest a table before me in the presence of mine enemies: thou anointest my head with oil; my cup runneth over. Surely goodness and mercy shall follow me all the days of my life: and I will dwell in the house of the Lord forever."

A. Simmons

Chapter Four

Finally, they arrived at the shop. Ruby thought it was over and Luke would just get out, but he didn't. He pulled out a cigarette lighter and begin to try to light things on fire in the car. "Stop Luke," Ruby screamed. "Just please get out of the car," she said. "I'm not going anywhere," Luke replied. He swung and hit Ruby in the head one last time. This time Ruby tried to put her hands up to protect herself, but it was too late. Blood was gushing out of Ruby's head.

Ruby began to scream. "What have you done! What have you done!" Ruby said.

Terrified for her life Ruby tried to get out of the car and run but Luke grabbed her and pulled her into the shop and locked the door. Ruby had left her phone in the car on the front seat. "That's what you get you bitch I'm going to kill you," Luke said. Blood was everywhere, and she wasn't sure how bad of a gash it was. Trembling and feeling faint, Ruby tried to act calm and sat down. *"Fear not them which kill the body but are not able to kill the soul: but rather fear him which is able to and destroy both soul and body in hell.* Matthew 10:28" she said to herself. Luke was pacing the floor. "Luke," Ruby said. "I'm going to be okay and we can try to work things out. I won't tell anyone this happened. Let's just got to the hospital and I'll say I fell." Luke paused for a moment. He turned and looked at Ruth, "You promise? Baby, I'm so sorry. I wasn't trying to hurt you," He said as he sat down beside her. "I know," Ruby said.

Luke helped Ruby up from the chair and proceeded to unlock the door. Ruby's heart was beating fast because she knew she had only told Luke that, so she could somehow escape. Her Jeep was parked right in front of the door. Her plan was to run out as soon as he opened the door and jump in her truck and pull off. "I love you," Luke said as he swung the door open to walk out. Ruby looked at Luke without saying a word and ran for her life. "You bitch" Luke said as he ran behind her.

Ruby jumped in the car and locked the door, but before she could reach the passenger lock Luke had run around the car and gotten in. Ruby grabbed her phone and jumped out of the car before Luke could get a good grip on her arm. Her shirt was completely bloody, and blood was running down her face. Ruby ran for the streets hoping someone would see her. Luke was close behind her but cautious not to touch her afraid someone would see. "Help!" Ruby yelled waving her hands. "Help!" One car zoomed past them. "Help!" Ruby screamed again hoping someone who lived nearby would hear her screams. She began to dial 911 on her phone. "Help me, please help me," she cried to the operator.

"I'm bleeding from my head. My ex is trying to kill me," Ruby said.

"What's the address of your location?" the operator asked.

"I can't see it, I don't know. My name is Ruby Smith from Lakeside and I'm at The Shop in Cedarbrook," Ruby said. "Ruby is that you? This is Lora. Just stay on the line I'm tracking your location."

Ruby was relieved that she knew the operator. "Please hurry," Ruby said. "He's standing about 20 feet away from me watching me."

"You're not going to get away," Luke screamed. "This girl is crazy she did this to herself," Luke continued.

Ruby was still near the street waving her hands and yelling help. Then a little black car Ruby thought she recognized came puttering down the street.

"HELP!!!" Ruby screamed waving her hands. It was Mr. Bailey the shop owner. Mr. Bailey pulled in the parking lot with disbelief on his face. "WHAT IS GOING ON?!" he yelled to Luke as he jumped out of his car.

"Lora, the owner of the shop just pulled up and is talking to him. I have to get out of here," said Ruby. "Ruby

I'm having a hard time tracking your call. The Police are trying to find you," said Lora. "Listen to me carefully Ruby," said Lora. "Are you still bleeding?" "I think so," said Ruby. "Can you make it to your car? What is going on now?" Lora asked. Without saying a word, Ruby saw Luke talking with Mr. Bailey and begin to slowly walk towards her car. "Ruby, Ruby are you still there," Lora asked. Ruby noticed Luke drop his head and she took off running to her car.

"Ruby, Ruby," said Lora. "What's going on? What's all that noise in phone? Is he chasing you? Talk to me Ruby. "Out of breath and safely in the car Ruby replied "I'm in my car. I'm going to try to make it to the police station." Luke looked up and realized Ruby was driving off and immediately started to chase the truck. Mr. Bailey tried to stop him, but Luke pulled away from his grip.

"Oh my God!" screamed Ruby.

"What's happening?" Lora asked.

"He's casing the car!" Ruby screamed "Lord Help Me!" Ruby slammed on the gas and Luke couldn't keep up.

"Ruby, are you safe? Is he still casing the car?" asked Lora.

"Yes, I'm safe," Ruby replied with an exhale. Ruby begin shouting "THANK YOU LORD," over and over again.

Ruby made it safely to the police station. She was greeted by her best friend Kimberly as she'd texted her to let her know what was going on. Kimberly reached her arms out to embrace Ruby when she walked in. "You did it, friend, you escaped," Kimberly said hugging her tightly. "You're safe now, the police are picking him up." "Thank you, friend," Ruby said. "I just don't understand how I keep allowing this to happen."

"That's why we're here friend. To help you understand," Kimberly said. The paramedics finished examining Ruby.

Luke had beaten her in the head so bad that he forced a bobby pin through her skull. Thankfully the cut wasn't too deep, and Ruby didn't need stitches. The paramedics patched her up and the ladies exited the police station. Blood and burned papers were everywhere in Ruby's car.

"I'm taking you back home with me," said Kimberly. "Do you want to just leave your car here?" she asked. "No, I want to drive it home. I feel like I need to," said Ruby. "I almost died in there and I need a reminder right now not to go back to Luke." "Are you sure?" Kimberly asked. "I'm sure," Ruby replied. Kimberly followed Ruby to her house where she left her car and grabbed clothes for the weekend. Thankfully she was able to sneak in without her family seeing her. This was one of the many incidents Luke and Ruby had. Each time Ruby went back. Even after being that close to death, the question still remained. Will she leave or go back? Ruby spent the car ride home crying and praying.

> *"Lord, I need your help right now. Why do I keep going back, Lord? You have delivered me and yet I went back again. I'm weak Father and I know I'm not supposed to be here but here I am. I feel stuck. You told me that I am your child and heir*

of your kingdom and yet I keep settling for less. Lord give me the strength to leave. I know you said in 2 Corinthians 12:9 that your grace is made perfect in my weakness. Most gladly, therefore, will I rather glory in my infirmities, that the power of Christ rest upon me. Lord, I stretch my hands to you right now. Let the power of Christ rest upon me Father. Thank you for your grace and mercy that keeps saving me. Lord help me not to rely on my own strength but yours and yours alone. Send your angels to be with me and protect me as I continue to try to escape. Deliver me father from whatever has me bonded to this abuse. Restore the brokenness inside of me Lord. Heal my broken heart Father. Help me find my mustard seed. In the mighty name of Jesus, I pray, Amen"

A. Simmons

Support:

"Love Should Liberate You"

Chapter Five

"Where there is no guidance a people falls, but in an abundance of counselors there is safety." Proverbs 11:14

"And now abideth faith, hope, and love these three; but the greatest of these three is love." 1 Corinthians 13:13

One of my favorite poets is none other than Maya Angelou. "MyLou" is what I like to call her. It may sound silly, but it makes me feel connected to her. What I wouldn't do to have one day to sit with her and listen! Born Marguerite Annie Johnson in St. Louis, Missouri on April 4, 1928 to Bailey and Vivian Johnson. Angelou's brother Bailey Jr. nicked named her "Maya" when she was 2 which derived from "My" or "Mya Sister."

Angelou was an American poet, singer, actress, memorialist, and civil rights activist. At the age of 3 her parents divorced, and she and her brother were taken to live with their grandmother in Stamps, Arkansas, by their father. About four years later, her father returned to Arkansas and took them back to St. Louis with her mother. Then tragedy happened for Angelou. At the age of 8, Angelou was raped by her mother's boyfriend Mr. Freeman. She confided in her brother and he told the family of the abuse. Mr. Freemen was jailed for one day and upon his release was murdered. After his murder, Angelou stayed mute for 5 years fearing that her voice had killed him and if she spoke again it could possibly kill someone else. Unfortunately, 1 and 3 women are victims of some form of abuse in their lifetime. (National Coalition Against Domestic Violence)

What's interesting about Angelou's silence is that just like physical and verbal abuse, the victim is left somehow feeling at fault for the abuse. However, it is not your fault! Fortunately, it was through her years of silence that she birthed the gifts of reading, memorizing, and observing the world around her. Sometimes God must call us out of the noise into the silence for our purpose in gifts to be born.

Many young girls of my time - if not all - at some point in our lives were inspired by one of her many quotes or poems. Several of her words apply to Support. Maybe you have heard her poem "Phenomenal Woman," or "Still I Rise." You may have had to recite it in your history class. Maybe you've read her books "Letters to My Daughters," or "I Know Why the Caged Bird Sings." Either way we've all been inspired by her or learned from her at some point in our lives. One of my favorite stories is a conversation between her and her mother. Of all the people and affirmation Angelou had received over the course of her life, the one that mattered the most was from her mom.

Angelou moved out with child at the age of 17. She would frequently go back and live with her mom when times got hard and her mother would always say the same thing when she returned: "Baby's home," with a smile. When she was 22 years old, her mom said something to her that would change her life. Angelou had just finished Sunday dinner at her mom's house. They both headed out for the street cart.

"You know I think you are one of the greatest women I've ever meet," her mother said. "Mary McCleod Bethune, Eleanor Roosevelt, and my mother: you are in that category."

Then she asked Angelou for a kiss. As Angelou got on the street cart she began to think of words her mother had spoken to her. She began to think: what if she is right about me? From that moment Angelou was free from the doubt of what she couldn't do or be and held on to words that her mother had spoken of what she could. After dealing with being raped, becoming a single mother at the age of 17, and any other obstacles she'd faced, her mother's love Liberated her.

Love liberates you and God is love. Liberates means to set (someone) free from a situation, especially imprisonment or slavery, in which liberty is severely restricted. Typically, when in an abusive relationship the abuser will try to isolate you from family and friends, but God said *"Where there is no guidance a people falls, but in an abundance of counselors there is safety"* Proverbs 11:14. Isolation provides them with power and control.

This is entrapment of the enemy because God said, "I have not given you the spirit of fear; but of power, and of love and of a sound mind." (2 Timothy 1:7) The abuser wants to isolate you and manipulate you into feeling like they have the power, but fret not God has given you the power. It is vital that you surround yourself with people who love and support you. It is through the strength and love God has given them that they will liberate you.

Chapter Six

"Ruby, you know you deserve better than this," said Kimberly.

"Yes, you do!" Jolie continued. "Do you realize how gorgeous you are?"

"Sister listen, you have people that love you. Do I need to call your brothers? He lucky I'm saved. I know you love him sister, but you know God is not the author of confusion but of peace," her sister Nichole said.

At this point Ruby had been kidnapped by her sister and friends. They'd all met up at Jolie's house and they meant business. She was scheduled to be the special guest performer at a poetry slam in New Orleans that day but had decided to cancel because she was depressed. However, her troop of confidants was not going to let that happen. Depressed and an emotional wreck, Ruby had once again found herself feeling defeated. She began to think of all the other abuse she had endured in the past.

The first time it happened he strangled her, kicked her out of moving car, and tried to run her over. She still went back. The time he punched her to the ground outside a hotel because he was upset. She still went back. The night she'd caught him with another girl that he claimed was only giving him a ride. She was so upset that she ran towards Luke and pushed him before they proceeded to fight (this time she fought back), and he choked her unconscious. She still went back. When he threatened to kill her and her family because she'd decided to leave. She still went back.

The president and co-founder of the National Family Justice Center Alliance, Casey Gwinn says that "Men who strangle women are the most dangerous men on the planet." Gwinn referenced to a study in the Journal of Emergency Medicine, that if a man chokes a woman once, he's 800 percent more likely to kill her during that relationship than if he assaulted

A. Simmons

her any other way (Blog at WordPress.com, Should The Victim Fight Back? By Kia Richardson). Luke had strangled Ruby twice, yet she still went back.

You would think Ruby would be ready to leave at this point but a part of her was still willing to take another chance. "I just need to fix whatever is going on with me," Ruby had convinced herself. Luke had already been in jail and Ruby had a protection order out against him, but she couldn't seem to let this toxic love go.

"Tonight, it's all about you," said Jolie. "We even got a us a chauffeur." Jolie had an all-white, brand new, fully loaded Suburban with tan leather seats.

"We saved the whole back seat just for you," Jolie continued.

"Guys, I don't think I can go speak in front of people tonight," Ruby said. "I'm not sure if I'm even worthy to be doing this at this point."

"No ma'am, we're not going allow you to feel like that, so you might as well snap out of it." her sister said.

"You should like Jeremiah." Nichole continued. "In Jeremiah 1:5-7, God told him before I formed thee in the belly I knew thee; and before thou camest forth out of the womb I sanctified thee and I ordained thee a prophet unto the nations. Then said Jeremiah Ah, Lord God! Behold, I cannot speak: for I am a child. But the Lord said unto me, say not, I am a child: for thou shalt go to all that I shall send thee, and whatsoever I command thee thou shalt speak."

"You better say it Nichole," Jolie chimed in.

"Amen, Amen," Kim said.

"Sister just like Jeremiah you are worthy," Nichole said. "Remember you are a child of a King, I don't care what Luke says."

"The devil is a Liar," Jolie shouted from the front seat.

A. Simmons

Ruby burst out in tears, "He's not that bad. He just needs a little help. I help people every day, he shouldn't be any different. I just don't think God is telling me to turn my back on him. I'm all that he has. He doesn't have a job, he's sleeping in a barbershop and he doesn't have a good relationship with his mother," Ruby explained. "I mean his own mother told me he was a liar and bipolar and not to deal with him. Whose mother does that?" Ruby asked. "I know he loves me and even though I'm not the only person he's done this to, I think with time he'll change for me." There was a silence in the vehicle.

"Wait, what do you mean he's done this to another person," Jolie said.

"So, Ruby found out through several resources that he's done this to another girl. She verified it through public records. Apparently, the girl had to move to another state," Kim said.

"He's already a felon for this?" Jolie asked.

"Yes ma'am," Kim replied.

"Can we please just not talk about this anymore guys?" Ruby asked.

"I agree!" Nichole said. "Let's just enjoy the rest of this night. We love you no matter what. Give me a hug." Nichole reaches across the backseat and gives Ruby a big embrace. Ruby rested her head on Nichole's shoulder for a moment and took a deep breath.

Ruby loved her sister Nichole and had admired her since she was a little girl. Nichole was the Vice President of a local bank as well as a Christian Author. If there was one thing she didn't play about it was her family and Ruby was her baby sister. Kimberly had known Ruby for several years, she'd worked with Ruby's mom for many years. Kimberly was a partner with Ruby's foundation. She was a community activist and the first African American female to own a ABA

A. Simmons

team (American Basketball Association). Jolie was new to Lakeside and had only known Ruby for the last 2yrs. She lived next door to Kimberly. She was a true crusader for Christ which is what their friendship what built own. She was a multimillion-dollar Insurance Agent, a pianist, and a wife and mother of 6 beautiful kids. They had vowed to support Ruby no matter what…and they meant it.

The rest of the ride was full of laughs and girl talk.

"We're here!" said Jolie.

"Okay guys I'm nervous," said Ruby.

"You got this sister," Nichole said.

They said a prayer and headed inside the venue.

Chapter Seven

The venue fulfilled all of Ruby's soul cravings. It was a dark candle light setting. The tables were covered with white table cloths and a single red rose in a vase. The music was soft, and Ruby had a VIP table right by a fireplace. Ladies and gentlemen, Ruby Smith has entered the building! Ruby smiled and waved as they took their seats. She wore a beautiful white and pink baby doll floral dress with a floral halo around her head. She opted out from wearing heels and chose some comfy gladiator sandals for the night. She took the stage. The lights were shining brightly in her eyes. Ruby asked the band to continue to play softly. She paused for a moment and began to speak:

He moves me, 1 totally consumes me as his love flows
Through me and poetic words soothe me
While his spiritual knowledge improves me
He moves me, 2 Like tidal waves in the sea
Or birds migrating east, together they form a soliterraneous chemistry

A. Simmons

And I become the sun to his earth and we create solar energy

He moves me, 3 baffles me, 4 Astounds me,
5 Turns my disbelief into beliefs, 6 My dreams into reality
Then he glides me across the galaxy
And I pass Mars, Pluto, Jupiter, And softly on Saturn's rings
Then I wish upon a shooting star that this man would marry me

He moves me, 7 Surely, he was sent to heaven
With a touch so powerful yet soft as a feather
And every night I thank God for sending me this fellow
Who's quite like Matthew, Mark, Luke, John, and Timothy
Sometimes I think he was born again just for me

He moves me, 8 And I find myself lost within his maze, yet found
Born to be, destined to meet
No longer I or me but rather We and us
Until we return to dirt or dust
And our heavenly father calls us home and opens his pearly gates for us

He moves me, 9 it's as if I've been hypnotized by his body's physique
That's physically stimulating my urethra, And with just the thought of penetration
I become most and weak, and now Niagara Falls literally

Falls from me.

He moves me, 10 And I can no longer pretend
Why am I running from this man?
Not being ready for the readiness he brought
Only indecisive thoughts of past situations
And present occupation and future destination
Instead of just simply appreciating this
Immaculate combination

He moves me 11
But my heart won't let me trust his intention,
What's his submission
And why are my imperfect imperfection, His perfect reflection
God, I don't want to love him in vain, and my heavenly
whispered He came in my name

He moves me and as the clock strikes 12
And this magical spell has finally run its course
And I find myself running back to my chariot and horse
But oh, what lamentation fell upon with just the thought of losing
the Father please forgive me, I know it must be he
The one to bring the magical glass slipper
That's sure to be the perfect fit
Because this Cinderella has finally found her prince.

A. Simmons

There was a standing ovation. Clapping and finger snaps

filled the room. You could hear her confidants shouting. "Way

to go Ruby!" Ruby took her seat with her heart full and tears

in her eyes. All her friends connected arms to give her a group

hug.

"That was amazing," Jolie said. "You are so talented."

"Thank you, guys," said Ruby. "The funny thing is I still

haven't found the man that I wrote that poem about. Luke is

definitely not him."

"Well Praise the Lord," Nichole said. They all laughed.

"Waiter can we get another round of wine?" Ruby asked.

"Coming right up."

They enjoyed the ambiance for another hour then

headed back to Lakeside. Reality begin to set in for Ruby.

She'd left her phone in the car and realized she had 96 missed

calls from Luke. She took a deep sigh and shook her head.

"This is crazy," she said.

"What's crazy," her sister asked.

"Luke has called me 96 times within the last hour," said Ruth.

"Wait 96 times?!" said Jolie.

"Ruby baby we love you, but he really needs to get some help and it's not your job to fix him."

"Please don't answer or call him back," said Kimberly. "Just cut the phone off."

"You guys are right I'm cutting my phone off. I'm not falling for it this time." Ruby said.

"Well, regardless if you go back or not we will always be here for you Ruby no matter what," said Kimberly.

"I know you said you love him sister, but I want you to think about what love is," Nichole continued.

> *"Love suffereth long and is kind; love envieth not: love*
> *vaunteth not itself, is not puffed up. Doth not behave itself*

A. Simmons

unseemly, seeketh not her own, is not easily provoked,

thinketh no evil; Rejoiceth not in iniquity, but rejoiceth in the

truth; Beareth all things, believeth all things, hopeth all

things, endureth all things. Love never faileth."

"And now abideth faith, hope, love these three; but the greatest of these is love, 1 Corinthians 13:13," continued Ruby. "Thank you, sister, for reminding me of that because Luke is none of those things."

"EXACTLY," said Kim.

Ruby began to cry. "You guys just don't know how grateful I am for each of you. I wish Tonya and Bernie was here as well. I feel ashamed, defeated, depressed, confused, and hurt. However, your friendship liberates me. It sets me free to be exactly who I am. It removes the guilt and shame. It eases my pain and even dries my tears. You guys give me strength and hope. You guys love me unconditionally. Your love liberates me and I'm utterly grateful. I almost died today at the hands of a man I keep running back to. One that has disrespected each of you to some degree and yet here you all stand; fighting with me. Thank you for not giving up on me," Ruby said.

She began to pray,

"Lord, Thank you for my support system. You said where there is no guidance a people falls, but in an abundance of counselors there is safety, Proverbs 11:14. Thank you Lord for safety. Thank you Lord for my confidants. Thank you Lord for their strength and their prayers. It is written that by grace are ye saved through faith; and that not of yourselves: it is the gift of God, Ephesians 2. Thank you, Lord, for this gift that has saved my life over and over again. Greater is he that is in me then he that is in the world. Help me to remember these words father as they sometime escape me. I rebuke any stronghold that keeps me bound to this broken

relationship. Deliver me, Father from the hands of my enemy.

Smite his head with fire. In Jesus' name, Amen."

The Make-Up

A. Simmons

Chapter Eight

I once meet a lady named Sunshine Johnson. She was sharing her testimony at a church I attended in San Francisco. Sunshine was a beautiful, divorced redheaded woman in her mid-40's. She had been married for over 15 years before she divorced her husband. They had met in college and dated for a few years before marrying. They shared two sons. Sunshine had been beaten, kicked, hit by her own car, shot in her arm (which she said was an accident), had a knife to her throat, raped, and verbally abused by the man she loved.

One day after her husband had nearly choked her unconscious, Sunshine decided to flee in the middle of the night to a family member's house. She was so afraid that she left the kids behind with no real plan of ever going back. She just wanted to get out! She'd been gone for a few days with no contact with her children. Her husband was calling all her friends and family frantically looking for her. Eventually he called Sunshine's cousin and she put him on speaker phone, so Sunshine could hear. He was begging and crying hysterically for answers. He talked about how much he missed her and couldn't live without her. After hearing his cries, Sunshine felt sorry. Hearing him sob reassured her that he loved her and things would get better so she went back. Like most, if not all, domestic violence cases things only got worse for her. After ten more years of abuse, Sunshine finally built up enough strength to leave. She was 35 years old. Sunshine had left a total of eight times before leaving for good.

The Assistant Director of Human Development and Family Studies at the University of Illinois, Jennifer Hardesty found that ultimately survivors want to be physically and emotionally connected again. This leads to victims returning to their abuser. Another factor to consider is most victims still love their abusers which can also play a major factor in them

A. Simmons

staying. Typically, victims do not want to leave their abuser, they just want the abuse to end. Not only is it extremely difficult for victims to leave an abusive relationship, it is dangerous. There is a 75% chance a victim will die trying to escape their abuser. Yes 75%! If there are firearms in the home, women are 8 times more likely to be killed.

According to Centers for Disease Control and Prevention, since 2003, over 18,000 women have been killed by domestic violence. Most people ask the question "Why won't they just leave?" To answer this question, I think we've covered a few examples already but let's go over a commonly used myth.

According to the Alabama Coalition Against Domestic Violence, people feel like battered women could leave if they wanted to. The fact is abusers deliberately isolate their partners, deprive them of jobs and opportunities for acquiring education and job skills. This, combined with unequal opportunities of women in general and lack of affordable child care, makes it extremely difficult for women to leave.

Another major factor to consider is "Belief." Sometimes she believes that according to the word of God the wife should submit to the husband and God would not forgive her if she leaves. She believes in God's covenant and thinks when she said, "to death do us part," and "for better or for worse," she is obligated to stay. Unfortunately, a victim will go back 7-10 times before they actually leave. This was only the 7th time for Ruby.

Chapter Nine

It had been exactly seven days and Ruby had managed to ignore Luke's phone calls and messages. She felt stronger than she had before and even though she still loved him, she resisted the urge to go back. Her plan was to keep her mind occupied with a busy schedule. Today she planned on having a mother-daughter day. It would be the first time they had been able to sit down together since that tragic day.

Ring… Ring… Ruby's phone begins to ring. She was sitting outside by the pool drinking mimosas with her mom enjoying the early morning sun. Ruby wore a two-piece pink swimsuit with a covering and Mrs. Lilly wore a fancy black one piece with a hat. "Who is it?" her mom asked. "If it's Luke please don't answer it Ruby."

"Trust me mom, I'm not," Ruby replied. "It's Tonya mommy," she said.

Tonya and Ruby weren't blood sisters, but they had always referred to each other as sister. They had known each other for about 10 years. Most if not all their conversation was centered around God. They were definitely soul sisters. Over the course of their friendship, Tonya had inspired Ruby to walk closer to God. Tonya was about 5'5" fair complexed and beautiful. She was the Vice President of a local hospital, a Christian Youth Leader at her church, Author and devoted wife and mother.

"Sister," Ruby said excitedly.

"Hey sister, where have you been?" Tonya said. "I have been trying to call you but your voicemail is full. I was starting to get worried. I haven't talked to you since everything happened," said Tonya. "I'm sorry, sis, it's probably all messages from Luke. I need to clear out my mailbox. I'm relaxing by the pool with mommy now," said Ruby.

"Okay, well you enjoy mommy and call me back a little later. If I don't hear from you I'll call you back. Love you sis," Tonya said. "Love you to sis," Ruby hung up and took a deep breath. "Mommy I really need to go through all these messages today," said Ruby.

"Baby do you think you're ready for that?" her mom asked, "You know you don't have to rush it." "I know mommy, but it's time," replied Ruby, "I'm going to do it later today." Ruby and her mom continued their day by the pool. They later slipped away for a few hours at the spa before grabbing Henry from school and going out to dinner. By the time they made it home, it was a little after 8pm. Ruby got Henry ready for bed and headed up to her room to reflect on her day.

Ruby took a long relaxing bubble bath to clear her mind before checking her messages. "Okay Ruby, you got this," she said. Ruby sat in the middle of her canopy bed cross-legged with her phone in her hand. She took a deep breath and start going through her messages. The first message was from Luke the same day he'd tried to kill her.

"Hey Ruby, I'm so sorry. I know words can't explain what I did, man that shit freaked me out so bad I'm so sorry Ruby. Wow. I'll never do it again. I'm so sorry. I'm so sick on my stomach that I did that to you. I'm so sorry. I'm sorry. I have to face the consequences now. The police have been up to the shop looking for me. I need to go down there and turn myself in. I really just wanted to tell you how truly sorry I am. That was uncalled for what I did to you. I can't make excuses, but I just got so much going on. I'm living in the shop, I don't have any money, and I'm dealing with a lot of personal stuff. I don't have anything but that is still no excuse for what I did. I apologize. It's just hard for me. The fact that I'm drinking doesn't help at all. I just need to get myself some help. I just wanted you to know that. Whatever happens to me I just want you to know that I'm sorry. I should've never said all that hurtful stuff to you. I'm sorry from the bottom of my heart Ruby. I love you forever no matter what. I'll never forget everything you've done for me. All the love you've given and tried to show me. I was just too caught up with thoughts in my head. Please just forgive me for what I did." End of message, the voicemail said.

Ruby began to cry. "Lord, I said I wasn't going to do this," she said. She continued to check messages. The next message was Luke calling from the jail.

"Ruby," Luke said while sobbing. "Please just answer my calls. They got me in here with some real criminals. I'm on the floor with murderers. I got jumped on last night. Please don't leave me in here. I know you still love me. I love you. Please just answer my call I don't think I can make it." End of message, the voicemail said. Ruby hung up the phone, balled

up in a knot, and cried herself to sleep.

Chapter Ten

The next morning, Ruby woke up to her phone ringing. It was the same number Luke had been calling from. Ruby answered the phone "Hello," said Ruby. "Baby it's me, please don't hang up." Luke said. "I'm so sorry baby please forgive me. I can't live my life without you," he said. "Please, please forgive me he begged." Ruby remained quiet for a moment then she began to cry. "Are you still there, hello?" said Luke. "Yes, I'm here. How could you do that to me Luke? You tried to kill me," said Ruby.

"Baby I'm so sorry I can't believe I did that to you. It will never happen again. Please forgive me. I'm scared and lonely. I got jumped on last night." The phone hung up. Luke's minutes had run out. He called right back but this time Ruby didn't answer. She needed a moment to think. She picked up the phone and called Tonya.

"Good morning sister," Ruby said.

"Good Morning SISTER!" Tonya said with excitement. "How are you?" she asked.

"Confused," replied Ruby. She begins to cry. "Sister I checked my messages and now I feel horrible. They are jumping on him in jail. I really think he's sorry and not going to do it again," explained Ruby.

"Sister you have no reason at all to feel bad. He always says he's sorry remember," Tonya said.

"I know sister, but I really think he is this time. I think being in jail is teaching him a lesson," said Ruby. "He sounded so pitiful on the phone."

"Did you physically talk to him or are you speaking of the voicemail?" Tonya asked.

"I took his call sister. I know I shouldn't have but I just couldn't help it after listening to his voicemail. God has forgiven me sister so why can't I do the same thing for him?" Ruby continued, "In Matthew 18:21-22 it says: Then came Peter to him, and said, Lord, how oft shall my brother sin against me, and I forgive him? Seven times? Jesus saith unto him, I say not unto thee, Until seven times: but, Until seventy times seven."

 Does this not apply to him sister?" Ruby asked.

A. Simmons

"Of course, it does sister, but forgiving him doesn't mean you have to be with him." Tonya replied. "Sister Genesis 1:27 says God created man in his own image, in the image of God he created him; male and female created he them," Tonya continued, "Do you really think God would create you in his image to be beat on? Then he made you joint heirs of his kingdom, sister." Tonya said. "Then to top it on off, John 14:12 says, 'Verily, verily I say unto you, He that believeth on me, the works that I do shall he do also; and greater works than these shall he do; because I go unto the Father.' Nowhere in the scriptures does God say he created you to be beat on sister," said Tonya.

"I know," replied Ruby. "Just keep praying for me sister because right now I feel like going back," Ruby said.
"Of course, I will. I'm going to call the others as well (Nichole, Kim, Jolie) so we can all be praying" said Tonya. "You know we love you Ruby," she said.

"I know, and I love you all too," Ruby hung up the phone and begin to pray.

> *"Lord can you hear me? Can you hear me Lord? Help me! I need*
>
> *your help. Why has my strength and faith escaped me? Why do I*

feel so weak and thrown away? Why do I feel like all of this is my fault? Help me Lord! My father who art in heaven hallow would be thy name. Thy kingdom come, thy will be done, on earth as it is in heaven. Give me this day father, my daily bread, and forgive me my debts as we forgive our debtors and lead me not into temptations but deliver me from evil for thine is the kingdom and the power and the glory forever and ever Father," Amen.

A. Simmons

Chapter Eleven

Over the next few days, Ruby started to take Luke phone calls from prison and before you know she was accepting him back. She even went as far as putting money on his books and paying for their phone calls. Every inch of her knew she was making the wrong choice. She hadn't really told her confidants that she'd planned on reuniting with Luke once he got out. They'd already been talking about finding a place to stay away from everyone to focus on their relationship. They weren't married yet but they'd started planning that as well. After spending 2 ½- 3 months in jail, Luke was bailed out by someone in his family. Ruby picked him up herself. Nobody knew where Ruby had disappeared to, and she wouldn't answer her phone for anyone.

"Kim, have you talked to Ruby," Jolie asked.

"No, I've been trying to contact her but I can't get her to answer," said Kim.

"Lord I hope see hasn't gone back to him," said Jolie.

"Let me call Bernie and see if she's heard from her," said Kim.

"Okay, call me back," Jolie said.

Bernie was the one friend that every girl has. She has a "No Tolerance for BS Policy," and will literally go to war for you. She owned her own make-up line as well as sunglasses line. She was extremely artsy and a celebrity in her own right and of course beautiful. Because of Bernie's love for Ruby, she couldn't just sit back and watch her hurt so she had distanced herself a little from the situation. She was still just a phone call away for Ruby and she texted her inspirational quotes almost every day.

"Hello," said Bernie.

"Hey Bernie, it's Kim. Have you talked to Ruby?" she asked.

"No why? What's wrong? You're scaring me. Do I need to be somewhere right now with my pistol?" Bernie said.

"As much as I wish I could say yes to the pistol, no you don't have to pull out. However, we haven't spoken with her and nobody can get in contact with her." Kim said.

"Oh wow," said Bernie. "Hold on one second let me check something out" she said. Bernie pulled up the local inmate search on her phone to see if Luke was still in jail and he wasn't.

"Kim I just searched Luke's name on the prison inmate search and his out," said Bernie.

"Oh no," Kim said. "She's probably somewhere with him."

"I can almost guarantee you she is. Let me know when to talk to her. I can't stand to see him do her like this. She deserves better," said Bernie.

"I will," replied Kimberly.

Kimberly quickly hung up the phone to call Jolie to tell her the news, then she calls Nichole.

"Hello," Nichole said.

"Nichole it's Kim. We have a problem. Luke is out of jail and we can't get in contact with Ruby. We have to go to our prayer closet and pray," said Kim.

"I had already started to pray earlier. I could just sense something wasn't right after I'd called several times and no answer," Nichole said. "I don't think she's in danger, but we do need to pray for her state of mind right now."

"I agree," said Kim.

"Okay, I'm going to call Tonya. I'll call you back if I hear anything else," said Nichole.

Before Nichole could call Tonya her phone rung. "Nichole where is Ruby?" asked Tonya.

"We think she is somewhere with Luke but none of us have been able to get her to answer," Nichole said.

"I knew she was going to go back after I we had that long talk. Lord please protect our sister," Tonya said, "I'm going to keep calling her until she answers. I'll call you back Nichole." The phone hung up.

Tonya called and called. If fact they all did but still no answer. Then Tonya decided to send her a message. "Sister I know you see us calling and its okay that you're not answering but know we are not calling to judge you. We are calling because we love you no matter what. We may not like the decision you've made but we love you either way. We're praying for you. You're a beautiful strong woman of God. No weapon formed against you shall prosper. Call me when you feel like talking." Within about 20 minutes Tonya got a phone call from Ruby.

"Hey sister, I'm too embarrassed to talk to anyone right now but I have decided to take Luke back. I'm not in danger. Thank you for sending me that message," said Ruby.

"You're welcome, sister, thank you for calling me back. Do you mind if I pray for Luke as well because he needs it?" asked Tonya.

"Absolutely," said Ruby.

"As a matter a fact what's his email address I'm going to send him something anonymously and copy you."

"Thank you, sister," Ruby said.

Ruby sent over their emails. About an hour passed and Ruby got an email alert on her phone. Ruby opened the message and begin to read.

"You don't know me, and I don't know you but when I envision whoever you are, I see you smiling. Have you smiled lately? I see beautiful eyes and a bright smile that express peace and happiness. Have you experienced peace and happiness lately? I see success, ministry, and you making a positive influence on young people. See you have a story that has not fully formulated yet because you are only half way through it. There is so much you will be able to attest to and say that 'Yes I've been there, done that, but God has restored me, transformed me, and elevated me to this place.' Your presence will encourage others and what you have to say will be heard, respected, and will reflect the heart of God. I don't care the state you are in now. I don't know it, but I do know that you matter, you serve a greater purpose, and that God wants to use you. See we all go through different things for different reasons but we either come out on one side or the other. There are two sides of everything: heaven and hell, good and evil, right and wrong, and we will end up on either side. What side do you feel you are on now and what side do you want to be on?

A. Simmons

I used to be in a dark place in my heart and mind once. I wanted to hurt people, myself, and my son. I didn't want to hear about God because I did not want to experience the power of God in that moment. I just wanted to pity myself. I would sulk in depression and wanted to just sit and not move one step out of the that low place because it called for too much effort. I had to put forth something. I had to change, and I was too lazy to do it. I got mad because God did not move the way I expected or wanted him to BUT all the while he was waiting with open arms for me. God loves you so much that he just waits patiently for you. He waits, and waits, and waits, but he can only wait so long. Because as he waits Satan is attacking our mind and spirit to keep us from experiencing the love, peace, happiness, joy, and loving kindness God has just sitting there for us at his feet.

Satan has a task to complete and while we are not working to establish or nurture our relationship with God, Satan is working to kill us. If you feel like you should be dead or want to be dead that is *only Satan saying, 'You will never make it to be who God has called you to be.' He's saying 'You will never see the success that God has for you in your future, you will never experience God,' because when you experience him, FOR REAL, your whole life changes. Not the type of change where things around you start changing immediately (and sometimes they do. God can do anything) but the type of change that YOU change, your mindset changes, your desires change, and you see yourself how God see you. God wants to see you prosper and have good success (3 John 1:2) and will give you provisions for that BUT YOU MUST SURRENDER your heart, your mind, and your SOUL to CHRIST. God loves you so much that he gave his son to die for your sins (John 3:16).*

You don't have to die in sin because Jesus bore all of our transgressions on the cross. I just encourage you to just cry out to God. Tell him you are sorry for all you have done to hurt him (because he hurts when we hurt ourselves and others mentally, physically, spiritually). Ask him to teach you patience, how to love, how to understand his WORD, and how to live a life pleasing to

A. Simmons

him. You can start fresh and I believe in you because GOD Does! I speak to every attack of the enemy (Satan) in your life and declare it NOT SO. You are not a failure, you will not die in sin, you will not be depressed, you will not be led by your emotions, you will not be confused by religion, you will not be ruled by spirits of doubt, fear, unbelief, envy, jealousy, murder, idolatry, lust, pride, sexual immorality, fits of rage, and drunkenness.

I speak deliverance from every kind of evil in your life in the name of JESUS (there is power in his name) I speak, joy, happiness, good success, prosperity, self-control, humility, integrity, patience, gentleness, and GOD'S LOVE in your life. I pray that his love overtakes you and transforms you from the inside out. For God to dwell in you he must cleanse and purify you first. I pray that your new walk in Christ be based on relationship with him and not on religion. In the end, we either suffer consequence (eternity in hell) or we are rewarded (eternity in heaven). LET GO and LET GOD! Ask for forgiveness and apologize to the people you have wronged and ask *for God to remove any unforgiveness in your heart, so you can move forward with your life… a Blessed life! I trust and believe that God is waiting for you to just say YES to him. I plead the blood of Jesus over you and cannot wait for what I have envisioned to become a reality. SMILE... JESUS LOVES YOU!*

Restoration and renewal are yours,

Someone concerned about lost souls… Be Blessed. "

Ruby fell to her knees after reading it and begin to praise God. Although the message was intended for Luke there was definitely some strongholds released in her life. Now she prayed that Luke would read it and receive it. Time would only tell.

A. Simmons

Yes, Verbal Abuse is Abuse

Chapter Twelve

"Death and life are in the power of the tongue: and they that love it shall eat the fruit thereof" Proverbs 18:21

"Out of the same mouth proceedeth blessing and cursing. My brethren, these things ought not so to be." James 3:10

I didn't know verbal abuse could be just as bad as physical abuse, if not worse. In the mid 1980's, I remember spending summer days and after school at my granddad's house. It was a white house with black shutters on the windows. The front porch was big enough to fit me and about 10 of my cousins at one time. Leading up to the porch was a long walkway with monkey grass on both sides. We spent many summer days playing in the front yard. My granddad had a garden in the back, so we didn't spend too much time back there. There were 3 bedrooms, one bathroom, a living room and a kitchen. To my mom and her siblings, it was their mansion growing up. There were twelve of them raised in the smallest, yet biggest, house you would ever see. I literally could not imagine them living there this day in time but it is still standing and filled with love.

One day my cousin and a close family friend were in the kitchen. It was a very small kitchen. There was just enough room for a stove, refrigerator, cabinets, and a kitchen table that sat four at a time. My cousin and our friend were having an argument. He told her she was ugly, and her response was "Sticks and Stones may break my bones, but words will never hurt me." At the age of 7, that was my first time hearing that statement and from that day forward I began to use it. I said it every time somebody would say hurtful things about me. If I didn't say it out loud I would whisper it to myself. It was my secret weapon. Growing up as a skinny dark-skinned girl with extra kinky hair wasn't easy. I still remember sitting in my 4th grade class like it was yesterday. My teacher Mrs. Abernathy, who is to this day still my favorite teacher. One of the guys in my class talked about my hair so bad that I got a Press and Curl when I got home. Almost 27yrs later and I still giggle when I think about it. Even though I cracked back it still hurt. As I got older I begin to realize that chanting the phrase was no longer working and words indeed do hurt. Not only do they hurt but they linger. Did you know that verbal abuse can poison your thoughts about you, leaving you feeling confused and in doubt? Let's dig a little deeper.

In April 2007, The Harvard Gazette published an article by William J. Cormie. Cormie reports that according to a Harvard University psychiatrist, the often-repeated children's rhyme "stick and stones my break my bones but names will never hurt me," is wrong. The report suggests that when verbal abuse is constant and severe, it creates a risk of post-traumatic stress disorder. The same type of psychological collapse experience by combat troops in Iraq. Wow! So, in actuality when trapped in a verbally abusive relationship, you're at war.

A. Simmons

Abusers can use verbal abuse to manipulate you, belittle you, shame you, hurt you, make you feel guilty and overall lower your self-esteem. They will even provoke "YOU," the "VICTIM" to become physical to defend yourself in some cases. Well, what do you do when the person you love is also the person who cuts you with their words?

For me, words are very important. I remember reading the book The Five Love Languages by Gary Chapman. It wasn't until I read that book that I realized just how much words meant to me, since Words of Affirmation is one of my love languages. Words of affirmation are important. Not only for me, but for every human being. Words that encourage build you up, not instill fear or tear you down. Literally every word we speak affects our mind. Did you know words that are not true, even if spoken, are true to our subconscious mind? The scripture tells us, "So as a man thinketh, so is he" (Proverbs

23:7). Perhaps the worst I heard from the person I loved was "You are worthless."

A few months had past, and things had only gotten worse between Ruby and Luke. Ruby tried everything in her power to help him. She had decided that they should move in together. She figured him living in "The Shop" was taking a toll on his mental health and they could form a stronger bond. It was quite the opposite. Ruby could barely talk on her phone without Luke accusing her of talking to someone else. It didn't matter if It was a boy or girl, friend or family, there was always an issue with Ruby being on her phone, period. "You give your friends too much access and control over you, and you don't think you should change that for me?" Luke would ask Ruby.

"If you had a problem with any of my friends I would stop talking to them," he said. Ruby constantly reassured Luke that she wasn't talking to anybody or leaving him, but it didn't work. The verbal abuse got worse and worse.

A. Simmons

Chapter Thirteen

It was a beautiful summer's day. Luke was working, and Henry was with his father. Her brother Ken had planned a 40th birthday party for her sister-in-law Winnie that day. Ruby and her mom spent all day that morning looking for Ruby something to wear that night. They had been everywhere. Finally, they went into a little boutique called Tulips. It was about 15 minutes outside of town and extremely vintage.

"Mom, I'm looking for something long and royal," said Ruby. "The event is at the Garden Winery so I'll need to dress it up a little bit." Ruby continued.

"How about this one sweetheart? It looks like you," Mrs. Lilly said.

"I love it," said Ruby. "Let me try it on." Ruby's mom had picked out a purple floor length backless dress with flowers on the front. It was beautiful and looked great on Ruby.

"What do you think mom?" Ruby asked.

"Oh, sweetheart it is beautiful," Mrs. Lilly replied. "You are just as beautiful as the first day I brought you home from the hospital."

"Aww, thanks mommy. I love you," said Ruby.

"I love you too sweetheart," her mom replied. Ruby purchased the dress before grabbing a quick bite to eat then heading home.

"Are you sure you don't want to come to the party after you leave work?" Ruby asked Luke.

"No thanks, I'll be fine," replied Luke. For whatever reason Luke was in a bad mood. He hated when Ruby went anywhere. He would often tell her "You just want attention, you slut." It didn't really matter where she was going, who she was with, or how she was dressed - his thought process was the same.

"Well I'll be there. If you change your mind just come. Otherwise I'll see you at home. Love you," said Ruby.

A. Simmons

"Yeah right," said Luke and hung up the phone. Ruby ignored his attitude and resisted the urge to call back.

Ruby looked gorgeous. The purple dress fitted her perfectly. She wore a diamond halo on her head and a simple pair of diamond slippers. "Okay mom, I'm leaving. How do I look," Ruby ask as she walked down the stair into the foyer. "Beautiful baby," her mom said. "Willie, Ruby's ready to go."

"You look beautiful mom," said Henry.

"Thank you, my sweet baby. Take care of grandma while I'm gone," said Ruby.

"Aww, okay," said Henry. "Why can't I go again?" Henry asked hugging Ruby. "It's not for kids, baby, your cousins are on their way over here too. You guys can have your own party. Grandma is going to make milkshakes. It will be fun," said Ruby. She kissed Henry on the forehead and left.

The venue was about 25 minutes away which her stepdad, Willie took her. She closed her eyes and prayed on the ride over that Luke's attitude would change by the time the party was over. Either way, Ruby was determined to have fun that night and that she did. She was one of the first people there. Her sister Nichole was at the door when she got there.

"Hey sister you look so pretty!" said Nichole.

"Thanks! So, do you sister," Ruby replied as she hugged Nichole.

"I just talked to your brother and he's about 15 minutes out from bringing Winnie," said Nichole.

"Ok, well let's go ahead and grab a glass of wine before they get here," replied Ruby. Nichole was happy they'd both gotten there a little early, so she could try to talk to Ruby about Luke.

"So, how are things between you and Luke. Have things changed any since you guys moved in together?" asked Nichole.

"To be honest, sister, things have gotten worse. I try not to bother you guys because it's been going on for so long now and I keep going back," replied Ruby.

"Well thank you for speaking for me," said Nichole sarcastically. "I never said I was tired sister and I NEVER will be tired of supporting you through this. However, let me say this: it's time for you to leave sister. We didn't say anything when you took this leap of faith moving in with Luke, but things have gotten worse and the next step is somebody getting really hurt," Nichole said.

"I know, I know. I'm actually getting tired myself sister. I don't think I can take being called a bitch and hoe, and how I'm a horrible mother, or fake, or gay, or constantly trying to prove my love to someone who doesn't love me," Ruby said.

"Well sister you know verbal abuse can be far worse than physical abuse," Nichole said.

"I know that now, I've actually started to believe some of the things he's said to me," said Ruby. "The other day he told me nobody was going to want a woman my age with a baby and I actually kind of believe him."

"Wait a minute," Nichole said laughing. "Sister, you're a model! I see about 3 different guys who haven't stop looking at you since we've been here and that's what you think? SNAP OUT of it sister! God's got something so much better for you. He's the one with the low self-esteem issues. I really don't like him and he's lucky I'm not a man because I would…, well I'm not going to go there. I'm saved now. However, you already know what your brothers want to do to him and it's only so much more they're going to be able to take before Luke gets hurt. I'm just saying," finished Nichole.

"I hear you sister. Thanks for that. I'm in a different head space then I was a few months ago and I'm really thinking about ending things. HELL, he better recognize what he got," Ruby said raising her glass for a toast. "Now let's take a toast to me SNAPPING OUT OF IT as you said," she said laughing. They click their wine glasses and got up from the bar to welcome the birthday girl in.

Chapter Fourteen

Winnie had been in Ruby's life since she was 15 years old. She was the ONLY girl that she's ever liked dating her brother. The day her brother brought Winnie home, Ruby was drawn to her. Not only was she beautiful with hair nearly to her butt, but she was extremely down to earth. They hit it off and before long Winnie had become more like her sister then her brother's girlfriend. Their relationship was so close that even her brother would get irritated with the loud concerts they would put on in her mom's basement. Everybody loved her, and she looked like Ruby's mom too. She knew all of Ruby's secrets! Ruby loved her so much that she'd become teary eyed hugging her when she walked in. "HAPPY BIRTHDAY TO THE BEST SISTER-IN-LAW A GAL COULD ASK FOR!" Ruby said full of emotion as she hugged her sister. "Thank you," said Winnie.

The party was everything Winnie could have asked for. Catered food, photographer, DJ, gifts, and family and friends. They had a ball! Ruby hadn't had this much fun in forever, mainly because Luke had begun to isolate her. She danced and danced. Especially her and Winnie. They sang Happy Birthday and gave speeches. What was supposed to be a 2-hour party lasted about 4 hours and nobody was ready to go at the end...but all good things must come to an end. Winnie gave her thanks to all her family and friends and they packed things up.

Ruby had planned on riding home with her brother that night since Luke had to work. She grabbed her phone from her purse to check in with Luke. To her surprise, Luke had called 20 times and she had about 10 messages.

"I'm sure you're having fun laughing in some guy's face," said Luke on one of the first messages.

"You're a real class act. You're so embarrassing," he said on another.

"I bet you're acting like a jezebel up in there," he said. The messages were so disgusting.

"Here we go with this," said Ruby, "I guess it's back to reality."

Ruby tried to call Luke, but he wasn't answering his phone. She tried a few times and said forget it. After having an amazing night Ruby just wanted to go. She grabbed the keys from her brother and told him she would be waiting in the truck.

"Are you okay?" her brother asked.

"Absolutely, brother. You did an amazing job. I'm just tired," Ruby replied. She didn't want to say anything to affect Winnie's day.

"Ok. I parked right in the front," her brother said. Ruby grabbed the keys and headed out to the truck. She tried to call Luke one last time but to her surprise he was already outside parked three cars behind her brother.

"Luke, I didn't know you were out here, baby," said Ruby as she opened the door to her truck. Luke's car was broken down so Ruby let him drive hers to work that night.

"Yeah, I bet you didn't. You think I'm crazy don't you," said Luke.

"Luke what are you talking about," replied Ruby.

"You can just go ahead and ride with whatever dude you had picking you up," he said.

"Luke, my brother was dropping me off at home. I tried to call to tell you that, but you didn't answer. I even have his keys in my hand," said Ruby. "Just wait right here while I take his keys back in. I'm riding with you," she said.

Ruby hurried back in to take her brother his keys and jumped back in the car with Luke.

"I'm ready," she said.

"So, did you call and cancel your ride?" said Luke.

"Luke, I don't want to argue with you. Nobody was taking me home, but my brother. Can you just stop it please?" Ruby asked.

Luke looked a Ruby with complete disgust in his eyes. "Ewww," said Luke. "What in the hell do you have on - you look like slut. Oh, I know you were in there hoeing," he said.

Ruby began to get upset but tried her best to remain calm. "Luke my mom picked this dress out. It's dragging the floor.

A. Simmons

The only skin that's showing is some of my back and arms and with my hair long you can't even see my back," said Ruby. "I don't look like a slut. I look like a Queen," she said.

"Queen my ass You thought you was going to get you some from somebody, tonight didn't you? Who was picking you up? Don't try to use your brother as a cover up," he said.

Ruby was baffled.

She was not expecting the night to end like this. "Listen Luke I wasn't doing anything wrong and again my mother picked out this dress. As a matter of fact, let's stop by there before we head to the town house," she said.

"Sure slut," he said.

Ruby had gone and bought her and Luke a condo. She figured she and Luke needed their own personal space for things to work. Luke had made her so upset that she was honestly thinking about not going to the condo with him that night. They pulled up at her house and Ruby jumped out and went in.

"What's wrong, baby?" her mom said as Ruby opened the door crying.

"Mom can you please go talk to Luke. He's talking about I look like a slut and I had someone picking me up from the party," said Ruby.

"Ruby you just need to stay here. This doesn't make any sense. He is crazy," her mom said.

"I don't want to stay here, mom. He might do something to the condo and he's in my truck. I tired of this mommy," said Ruby.

"Baby I'm worried about you going with him; he might try to kill you this time," her mom said.

"Trust me mommy I'll be fine. God's got me. I promise I'm getting tired of Luke. I can't help him. Just please walk out there with me. Maybe he'll calm down if you talk to him," said Ruby.

Upset and hesitant, Ruby's mom slipped on her slippers and they walked out to the truck.

"Hey Luke," she said. "Ruby told me you didn't like her dress, but I picked that dress out Luke and there is absolutely nothing wrong with it. Also, her brother was bringing her here to wait for you," she said.

"I'm not sure why she even brought you out here Mrs. Lilly, we are good," said Luke.

"NO, we are not good. You just made a big deal about my dress calling me a slut and insisting that I was waiting to be picked up like some hooker. Don't try to act innocent now that my mom is here," said Ruby.

"Luke," her mom said, "Just let it go and you guys go home and go in separate rooms if you have to, but no more name calling or arguing, and definitely don't put your hands on her," Mrs. Lilly said.

"It's not me, it's him mommy," said Ruby.

"Baby just let it go," she said.

"We're straight, Mrs. Lilly," said Luke and they pulled off.

"I don't know why you brought your mom out here. I don't give a damn what she says or nobody else. You look like a slut whore and you had some dude picking you up," said Luke.

"Just back up and take me back because you're not going to stop," Ruby asked.

"I'm not taking you nowhere," Luke said. Ruby could see her mom's reflection in the mirror. She was still standing in the yard.

"I should've listened to you mom," Ruby said to herself.

"Lord please let me make it through the night," she prayed. Against her better judgment, Mrs. Lilly watched her daughter ride off with the same man that tried to kill her three months ago.

Enough is Enough

Chapter Fifteen

I imagine on Dec. 1, 1955 a little lady by the name of Rosa Parks was thinking "Enough is Enough." I agree with her when she said "There is only so much hurt, disappointment and oppression one can take. The line between reason and madness grows thinner," Rosa wrote in one of her articles recently filed in the Library of Congress, on display for the next decade. Many thought Rosa was the timid and passive little lady who was simply tired that day she refused to give up her seat on the bus to a white passenger, but it was so much more.

Born Rosa Louise McCulley on February 4, 1913, Rosa Parks was a seamstress at the Montgomery Fair Department Store. She had seen a lot and done a lot in her lifetime. As a young child she watched her grandfather stand guard over their family because, at any moment the KKK could come and burn down their house and them. She was forced to walk to school because the elementary school bus would only carry

A. Simmons

white kids. She experienced the separation of white and colored bathrooms, water fountains, seats and the lines. At the age of 19 she met her husband Raymond Parker, a civil rights activist and member of the NAACP. In 1932 they married, and Rosa McCulley became Rosa Parks. Soon after, she joined her husband as a secretary and youth leader in their chapter of the NAACP. Yes, Rosa Parks fight for freedom started long before she refused to give up her sit.

She died Oct. 24, 2005 and was the first woman and second African American to be laid to rest at the US Capitol Rotunda. Amongst many other awards and accolades, she was presented the Medal of Freedom by former President Bill Clinton. In Dec. of 1955, Dr. Martin Luther King Jr. led a 381-day bus boycott in Montgomery from what most people assumed stemmed from a little lady who refused to give up her seat because she was "tired" and her "feet hurt." Indeed, Mrs. Parks was tired.

On a single slip of crumbled-up yellow paper, Rosa wrote "I had been pushed around all my life and I felt in that moment I couldn't take it anymore." Like all of us Mrs. Parks hit that defining moment in her life when "ENOUGH IS ENOUGH."

Chapter Sixteen

Ruby and Luke made it safely to the condo. He had blasted the music loud all the way home. He typically liked to play music that was degrading towards Ruby. This time he played a rape song called "These Hoes at Loyal." Ruby kept quiet and ignored him. When they got to the house Ruby immediately went into Henry's room. She closed the door and put on some gospel music. Luke wouldn't let it go. He kept opening the door to the room and blasting the same song he did in the car. Finally, Ruby got up.

"You just won't leave it alone will you, Luke?" Ruby demanded.

She went and unplugged her speakers that Luke had blasting the music really loud. "I don't care if you play the music Luke, but we can't disturb the neighbors with the noise," she said.

"Don't get mad cause you a hoe. You ain't nothing but the devil," said Luke.

"I really don't care what you say about me, Luke," replied Ruby.

"Oh, I know you don't because you were about to go be laid up with another dude tonight anyway. Talking about you a Christian." Luke said laughing. "Freak hoe, Freak hoe," Luke said laughing and singing.

It took everything in Ruby's power to ignore him. She just kept saying to herself "The devil is a liar." This made Luke angrier. She continued to unplug her speakers, but Luke began to try and take them out of her hands. She tried to slip into the bathroom and close the door, but Luke kicked the door in.

The condo was about 2,000 square feet. It was upstairs and downstairs. Downstairs there was a bathroom, kitchen with a bar area, living room for entertaining, and a sunroom with a jacuzzi just off the living room. Upstairs held two bedrooms: the master bedroom with a walk-in closet and Henry's room, with a bathroom in the middle. Luke and Ruby began to tussle over the speakers. "I'm not putting up with this anymore if I have to fight for my life tonight, I will." Ruby told Luke. Luke grabbed Ruby by the arm and threw her to the floor.

They were right by the stairs. "You think you better than me," Luke yelled at Ruby. "I'll kill you for real." Luke had Ruby pinned down on the floor. "You ain't no real woman. Do your son know you a hoe?" said Luke. Ruby used all her might to try to get Luke off of her. She was kicking and trying push him off. She managed to get up, but Luke hit her in the face so hard she fell back on the floor and then he kicked her in the face. Ruby grabbed her face.

"WHY DID YOU DO THAT!" she yelled. "That's what you deserve after how you been embarrassing me. I'm going to treat you like a dog." said Luke. They were still at the top of the stairs. Ruby tried to get up again, but this time Luke pushed her down the stairs. Ruby's adrenaline was rushing so fast that she didn't feel anything. She quickly got up. Luke was coming down the stairs with a pair of scissors in his hand.

"I'm calling the Police," she said.

"Go ahead and call, I'll kill you before they get here," Luke replied.

In that moment Ruby was scared for her life. She believed that he would kill her. She believed that he didn't care if she was died or alive. She began to panic.

"I thought you said you loved me. Now you're going to kill me." said Ruby. "Lord please help me. Please help me Lord." Ruby was sitting on the floor with her phone in her hand. "Give me that phone. You ain't calling nobody. I don't love no hoe," said Luke. Ruby got up off the floor and went and sat on the sofa. She was already trying to fight back but that was only making it worse. Luke was much stronger than she was. At this point she believed that Luke would try to kill her, so she remained silent from then on.

Luke however was still talking. "Look at you... Where is your God now? You think you can just play me and nothing is going to happen to you," said Luke. Ruby just sat there looking at him. "I'm done wasting my breath on you," said Luke, "You don't know how to be a woman let alone a wife," Luke said. Luke walked back upstairs to the bedroom and closed the door. Ruby waited for about 30 minutes before she got up. She walked up the stairs to see if Luke had fallen asleep. Thank God he had. Ruby found the scissors beside the bed, so she grabbed those and went back downstairs. She pulled out her journal and started to write.

"Ruby, where are you? You must pull yourself together right now. You deserve better. You are better. I can't believe I've chosen to be with someone like him for so long. I've never had anyone treat me like this. I was trying to give it my all. I went over and beyond to help him. Supported him when his family turned their backs on him, gave him money when he didn't have a job, bought us a place of our own so he wouldn't have to continue to sleep in a barber shop. I basically did whatever I could in my power to help him and it was still not enough. I tried. I just can't see myself putting up with this abuse anymore. I know he needs help, but I can no longer be his punching bag or escape goat for all his emotion. Lord help me leave. Whatever it is that I need to do I'm willing, Lord. I can't take this anymore. My son needs me more now than ever. I am losing myself and the only person I should be dying for is you. The only person I should be chasing after is you. This time I am leaving and I'm not turning back. Enough is Enough! So, let me just breath…"

Sometimes exhaling is the hardest thing to do
When love had failed you
Escaped your embrace
And now tears flow from your face

A. Simmons

Taking you to a place of grief

Leaving you feeling like a lonely castaway at sea

While still clinging to love's toxic memories

Because love got the best of me

Or has just been put on repeat

Hypnotizing me,

Clouding my vision to see

Making me believe it's okay for this man to beat on me

Camouflaging what love should be

As my heart tick tocks to his lust beat

So, let me just breath

Cause I can't shake this feeling of needing love

Even after being beaten it's still my reason for being: LOVE

The meaning of my soul LOVE

LOVE controls

My walk, My talk

My wants, My needs,

It's my Motivation

My stimulation for penetration

And it's seeping through my skin

Creeping within

Flowing through my veins

Speaking to my brain

And softly whispering in my ear

No matter what Luke has done to you LOVE still lives here

So, let me just breath

The bible tells me that God is LOVE

And he lives in me

So, I am LOVE

And LOVE is me

I'm totally consumed properly groomed

Dressed to impress with LOVE engraved on my wrist

Even a blind man can see that I'm enamored with LOVE

And all that it does

And all that it means

But this time I picked a bad seed

He must be from the garden of Eve

Because surely the serpent has been persuading me

To eat, dream, and believe that Luke was for me.

So, Let me just breath

Because my heavenly father said

Love is the greatest thing in world

I like to think it's as beautiful as an oyster pearl

It outweighs faith and hope

It's the perfect antidote that coats my pain

Erases my shame

It does not blame, beat, envy or boast

Which lets me know lust must have gotten the best of me

A. Simmons

But Enough is Enough I'm ready to be free.......

Chapter Seventeen

Morning came, and Ruby was woken up by her phone ringing. She picked up the phone. "Ruby baby I have been calling you all night. I couldn't sleep. Are you okay," said the frantic voice on the other end. It was Ruby's mom.

"I'm good mommy. Last night was horrible. Luke threatened to kill me. My lip is busted, and my arm is bruised, but I'm okay mommy," said Ruby.

"No, you're not okay and this is not okay," her mom said.

"Mom trust me I'm fine. I'm planning to leave. I need you to help me. I don't know how yet but I will," said Ruby. "Okay baby whatever I need to do I will. Where is Luke now?" her mom asked.

"He's upstairs sleeping. I'll be home in a little while. Love you mommy. See you soon," said Ruby. "Love you to baby. Please call me if anything else happens," said Mrs. Smith.

Ruby headed upstairs to take a shower. To her surprise Luke was up, fully dressed standing in the bedroom doorway.

A. Simmons

"Good morning," Ruby said.

"Can you take me to the shop," asked Luke.

Ruby was a little hesitant, but she whispered to herself "No weapon formed against me shall prosper." "Yes, are you ready now," she replied.

"Yelp, I'm sure you need to see old dude from last night," he said.

The only response Ruby had to Luke was "I'm ready." They headed out to the barbershop. This time she let Luke drive. Luke controlled the radio again blasting the same crazy music. Ruby didn't say one word she was too busy thinking about how she was finally going to break free from him. She couldn't wait to drop Luke off to call her friends.

Finally, they made it to the shop. Luke grabbed his bookbag and jumped out. "Don't worry about me, I'm straight," he said slamming the door. Ruby knew what that meant. Usually Luke said this to try to manipulate Ruby into feeling sorry for him, however, this time Ruby was thinking

"Don't worry I'm not." Ruby crawled across the seat and

drove off. She immediately called her sister Nichole.

"Good morning sister," Nichole said.

"Good morning sis," replied Ruby. "I'm ready to leave Luke,

sister. I know I've said it before in the past but this time I've

had enough, sister. Last night was horrible. I have a busted

lip and bruised shoulder. He grabbed a pair a scissors and

told me if I called the police he would kill me before they got

there. I believed him, sister," said Ruby. There was complete

silence on the phone. "Sister, are you there?" asked Ruby.

"Yes, I'm here. The question is where Luke is. I've had about

enough of him myself," Nichole replied.

"I just dropped him off at the shop," said Ruby.

"Oh, ok," said Nichole, "what's the name of the shop again,"

Nichole asked.

A. Simmons

"Sister, I'm not telling you. Just know that I'm done, sister. I don't want to get you guys involved. I must come up with a plan. Please just pray that God will show me way," said Ruby.

"I will, baby sis. I'm so happy you have decided to leave. I knew that God would deliver you soon," Nichole said.

Ruby spent the rest of her day talking with her friends about leaving Luke. She asked each of them to pray for her strength to not go back. She knew this all-so-familiar feeling of "Enough is Enough." What was she going to do when she felt lonely? How was she going to react when she began to miss him as she had in the past? How would she resist thinking about what they could have had? What if she was giving up on him too soon and another woman reaped from all the work she had put in? Finally, what was she going to say when he called crying and confessing his love to her? Of course, he did.

Chapter Eighteen

Luke only stayed gone for a day before he returned. Luke did his usual routine of being overly nice for about a week. "I can't live without you," he told Ruby. "I need to get some help," he said. "We just need to get some counseling," he continued, "I've never loved a woman as much as I love you." It was if someone had put a record on repeat. Thankfully Ruby wasn't moved by it this time. She kept remembering him say "If you call the police, I'll kill you before they get her." She remembered all the names he had just called her just a few days prior to him praising her. This time it wasn't working. She played the role for the next few weeks and it wasn't easy.

The next incident happened when Ruby decided to go to a football game with her god daughter Lauren. Laruen was only 14 years younger than Ruby, so most people thought they were sister. She was gorgeous. She was about 5'7' fair skinned with waist length jet black straight hair. She'd

A. Simmons

followed in Ruby's footstep and had become a professional model and nurses. Even though Luke called Ruby and could hear Lauren in the back ground, he insisted that Ruby was out cheating.

"What you think I'm dumb or something," Luke said. "I knew you was nothing but a hoe, talking about you were at the game with Lauren." "Yeah you are a real live slut," Luke continued. "Talking about you a Christian." Luke bust out laughing, "You're more like a jezebel or a jinni. You like that attention don't you Mrs. Hollywood?" Luke went on and on, but Ruby didn't say a word. Instead she slipped out the front door and left. She refused to stay and listen to Luke's verbal abuse and it was only a matter of time before things got physical. Ruby jumped in the car and headed to her house in Lakeside. "Lord please, please show me a way to get out," prayed Ruby.

Ruby waited until the next day when Luke had gone to work before she went back to the condo. Her mind was racing. How was she going to leave? She thought to herself. Should she just pack up everything and leave then? Ruby didn't know what to do but what she did know was that if she wanted to live she had to leave Luke.

Ruby begin to think of a time in her life when she was believing God for something. She was living in LA and was thirsty for a closer relationship with God. She'd never fasted before and prayed for God to show her how to. God lead her to the ten-day Daniel fast where she only ate fruit and veggies. It was the best decision Ruby had ever made as God answered so many of her prayers. "God, I think it's time for me to fast again," Ruby said to herself. That day Ruby decided to do a 7 day fast praying that God would show her how to leave.

The first few days of Ruby's fast was a breeze. Mainly because she'd stayed away from the house during the day time and Luke worked at night. She studied the book of

A. Simmons

Danial and spent a lot of time reading Psalms. The rules of the fast was that Ruby could only eat fruit and vegetables and couldn't allow Luke to touch her intimately. Luke had no idea Ruby was fasting all he knew was she was acting distance. He had been trying to be nice to Ruby for some odd reason, but she wasn't falling for it. Day four however things started to change.

Chapter Nineteen

Day 4- Luke had taken the day off and pretty much stayed around the house all day. Ruby believes he could sense the distance. Ruby had gone to work and retuned home around 4pm. To her surprise, Luke was at home when she walked in. He never told her he wasn't going to work. She quietly came in and went to the kitchen to fix her something to eat. Luke was laying on the sofa in a T-Shirt and underwear watching TV.

"Hey baby how was your day?" said Luke.

"It was good," replied Ruby "I wasn't expecting you to be her right now."

"Yeah, I figured I'd take the day off to see what you had going on," he said. "You sure have been acting funny these past few days. Is there something you need to tell me," asked Luke?

"Nope I'm good," replied Ruby.

"Well you haven't touched me in days usually you're more affectionate then this," said Luke.

A. Simmons

"I'm fasting right now," replied Ruby.

"Oh, so fasting means you can't touch me," Luke replied.

He got up and walked over into the kitchen were Ruby was preparing her food and stood behind.

"Yes, it does. Please don't touch me Luke," replied Ruby.

"I can do what I want to do," he said.

"So, what you're saying is you're going to disrespect my fast?" she asked.

Luke laughs out loud "Go ahead you probably need to fast to get some of those slut ways out of you," he said.

"I was just waiting on the real Luke to show up," Ruby said. She stopped fixing her food and went upstairs. She knew it wasn't going to work being there with Luke, so slipped on some more comfortable clothes and headed back down stairs. Luke was back on the sofa watching TV.

"I'm headed over to my mom's to help her with something," said Ruby with her hand on the door.

"Yeah I bet you are. You can just drop me off at the shop. I took off to spend time with you, but I see you had other plans," replied Luke.

"Sure, I'll be in the car waiting," she said.

Ruby headed out to the car. She waited about 10 minutes before Luke came out with his back pack. Other than Luke looking like the Grinch the whole time, it was a peaceful ride. Ruby played gospel music the entire time. They pulled up to the shop and Luke jumped out angrily. He slammed the door and walked around to Ruby's window.

"You don't have to come get me tonight, I'm going to sleep at The Shop," he said.

"Are you sure," replied Ruby.

"YES! You are what you are," he said.

Ruby didn't even respond she just rolled up the window and pulled off. This was usually Luke's way of starting an argument, but she ignored it. She decided to stay in Lakeside that night and went to bible study with Kimberly and Jolie.

A. Simmons

Chapter Twenty

Bible study was amazing. It was actually a small group at Jolie's house. Kimberly had called Ruby when she was headed to Lakeside and told her she was going to pick her up. They all gathered around Jolie's dining room table. Jolie had a big family and probably the biggest dinning room table Ruby had ever seen, other than the on pictured in the Passover.

"How is your fast going," asked Jolie

"It's going well. Luke just had one of his moments today but I'm not going to let it affect me. I've been spending a lot of time away from the house and meditating," replied Ruby

"I'm so proud of where you are right now," said Jolie. "Just don't give up. Think about Daniel and what he was faced with when he refused to eat the Kings meat and drink the Kings wine. They were forced into the lion's den. A place where it was impossible to live. Not only did he live, but he came out without a SCRATCH!"

"It's almost over and we're right here with you," said Kimberly.

"Thanks guys for all your love and support. Today is day 4. I'm still not sure how and when I'm going to leave. I'm just going to trust God to lead the way. I love you guys," said Ruby.

"We love you too," said Jolie and Kimberly.

Kimberly and Ruby gathered their things and headed back to Lakeside to drop her off. It was only 8:30, which was still fairly early when Ruby got home but she was exhausted. She said a few words to her mom before she fell asleep.

Day-5 Ruby woke up to the smell of turkey bacon. Her mom was down stairs preparing breakfast. It was already 7:30am and Ruby needed to be in the office by 9am. She reached for her phone and realized she had 26 missed phone calls from Luke. She threw on one of her foundation T-shirts and headed downstairs.

"Morning mommy," said Ruby.

A. Simmons

"Good Morning sweetheart," Mrs. Lilly replied. "How did you rest last night?" she asked.

"I actually got some of the best rest I've had in a while. I'm getting stronger and slowly finding peace," Ruby replied. Ruby was sitting at the table eating her breakfast. Her mom set down beside her.

"Good. I didn't want to wake you, but Luke called my phone 5 times last night. When are you finally going to be done with him baby?" she asked. "You deserve so much better Ruby."

"Mommy I know. Sometimes love just gets the best of you and it knocks you down so hard it takes a while to get back it. I had been in a sunken place for a while mommy, but I've been delivered. I'm fasting right now to leave him. This time I'm not going back momma," said Ruby. "I promise."

Ruby's mom smiled and gave Ruby a big hug. "I love you baby, and I believe you can do this," she said.

"Thank you, mommy. I'll call you once I leave the shelter, replied Ruby.

"Okay baby," she said.

Ruby grabbed her keys and purse and headed to the car. She still hadn't check any of the messages Luke left so she took a moment to glance over them before she pulled off.

"I see you are with your boo tonight," said Luke via text. "I don't know why I even waste my time with you. You left me at the shop last night knowing I was hungry," he said. "I called your mommy phone looking for you to, but she didn't answer so don't try to lie and say you were with her. You are a real low life for leaving me down here."

Luke's nasty message didn't even effect Ruby. She simply replied, "Hey Luke sorry I was sleep when you called. Do you need me to pick you up when I get off?" Ruby asked.

"Yeah, I'll be here," replied Luke.

"Okay, I'll be there around 2," replied Ruby.

Ruby looked up at the ceiling and begin to pray. "Lord it's day 5. I'm ready and willing to leave Father just show me what to do." Ruby slide her phone down in her purse and left for work.

Chapter Twenty-One

Ruby arrived at 2pm as promised to pick Luke up from the shop. He got in the car and neither one of them said a word to one another. About 5 minutes in Luke started to talk.

"I have to be to work at 4, so I'm dropping you off," he said.

"No problem," replied Ruby.

"You sure?" asked Luke. "I figured you'd need it to see your boo since that's where you were last night," he said.

"Luke, I was at my mommy's house, but I'm not about to argue with you," she said.

"I know you're not because you know I'm telling the truth," he said.

They pulled up at the Condo and Ruby got out. Before she could unlock the door and get in, Luke had jumped into the driver's seat and sped off. Ruby went in and spent the rest of the night meditating. She knew it would be at least midnight before Luke got home so she took advantage of time. Ruby filled the tub with bubbles and took a long bath before heading to bed. She didn't hear from Luke until the next morning when he came in around 2am.

Day 6- It was Friday, surprisingly, Luke didn't try to touch Ruby when he got in the bed. He did however try to hold her hand, which Ruby allowed for a moment but slowly slipped away when Luke went to sleep. Ruby was off on Fridays, so she'd planned on spending the day resting and meditating.

She woke up at about 6:30 in the morning. Luke was still sleeping so Ruby slipped out of bed and went downstairs. She put on a pot of tea and boiled some eggs and made peanut butter toast. Since Luke was still sleeping, Ruby was able to do her morning meditation in peace. She went into the sunroom and kneeled down to pray, "Lord thank you for the gift of this fast. Thank you for your grace and mercy. Thank you for protecting and renewing my strength. Today is day 6 Father and I'm waiting to hear from you. In Jesus name. Amen."

Ruby got up and headed back in to fix her tea. When she walked in the door Luke was standing in the kitchen. "I see you're up early this morning," he said. "I've also noticed that you've been getting up early everyday lately. You leave the house and I don't see you until night time. I'm know I'm not perfect, but I love you and I'm sorry for the things I've done to you."

Ruby almost smiled but she stopped herself. The one thing that humans desire is an apology from someone who has hurt them however, Ruby wasn't falling for it this time. "I told you I'd been fasting," she replied.

"I know you have but just don't leave me; I'd be lost without you," Luke said walking up to Ruby.

He kissed her on her forehead. "You're the only person I have, baby."

A. Simmons

To avoid confrontation, Ruby hugged Luke back and said, "I love you, too."

Luke was trying to be extra nice, but again Ruby wasn't giving in. Not this time. She'd had ENOUGH! He knew that something was up, but he wasn't sure what.

"What are your plans for today?" asked Luke.

Originally Ruby had planned to stay in but quickly changed that when she realized Luke was trying to spend time with her. "I need to go pay some bills and get my hair done," replied Ruby.

"Okay, well I guess I can go to the shop and when you get done maybe we can get something to eat," he said.

"Okay," replied Ruby.

They both took showers got dressed and headed out. It was beautiful outside. Luke wanted to stop by a few stores before being dropped off. Ruby didn't object; she'd let Luke drive anyway. They finally got to the shop around lunch time.

"All right, have a good day baby," said Luke.

"Same to you," replied Ruby.

"What time will you be back?" he asked.

"I'm not sure but I'll call you when I'm on my way," she said.

Luke kissed Ruby on the cheek and she pulled off.

"Lord, the devil thinks he is so slick! Now that I'm trying to leave, Luke is being extra nice. Well, it's not working this time," she said. Ruby did go pay a few bills but didn't go get her hair done. Instead she spent a few hours walking around at a nearby park. She didn't want any distraction so she didn't take calls from anyone. Ruby found a Cherry blossom tree, which was her favorite and sat under it leaning back on its foundation.

This park had horseback riding, canoeing, paddle boats, hiking trails, zip lining, and plenty of space for picnics. Ruby sat under that tree for hours falling asleep at times. Usually she'd write in her journal, but not this time. She just enjoyed being in a peaceful place. Nature always made Ruby feel closer to God. In the distance, she could see what appeared to be a group of people holding hands praying. Although she wanted to join in, she didn't. In that moment she realized she needed to find a prayer service she could attend that day. She couldn't think of any churches that had Friday prayer services, so she pulled out her phone to google "Friday prayer services near me." Luckily, she found one. The prayer services started at 6pm. It was now 4:30pm. She had just enough time to grab a bite to eat and make it to the prayer service. She texted Luke to let him know there was a change in plans.

"Hey, I'm going to go to a prayer service at 6pm," said Ruby.

"So, what about dinner tonight?" asked Luke. "I thought we were supposed to be grabbing a bite to eat," he said.

"We can after prayer service if you want to," replied Ruby.

"Man, I'm sick of your shit. Go ahead and be with the people you love because it's definitely not me. Smh." said Luke.

"Okay," replied Ruby.

Ruby didn't argue with Luke. Instead she pulled the directions up in her phone and headed over to church.

Chapter Twenty-Two

Ruby grabbed a smoothie on the way to the Church. She had never been to the church before and was sure she wouldn't know anyone, but she didn't care. All she needed was an altar. When she arrived at the church there were only a few cars in the parking lot. Judging by the design of the building, the church had been there for many years. It was an all brown brick building with stained-glass windows. The entrance had two tall white wooden French doors. It was around 6,000 square feet in size. Ruby parked her car and went in. She was a little worried that she was underdressed as she only had on jeans and a T-shirt, but she wasn't going to let that stop her.

She was greeted at the door with a smiling face.

"Welcome to Grace Temple, how are you?" the lady asked.

"I'm doing well. Thank you," replied Ruby. "Are you guys having prayer service here tonight?" she asked.

"Yes, ma'am we are. You can go right through those doors into the sanctuary and pray wherever you like," she said.

"Thank you," replied Ruby.

Ruby took a deep breath and walked in. There were about three columns of pews, a balcony, and a long alter that wrapped around the pulpit and choir. Ruby went straight to the altar and fell on her face and began to pray:

Father, I pray that you release me from the strongholds from Satan that has me bonded to this abuse. The spirit of depression, guilt, shame, unworthiness, doubt, fear of man, lust, disobedience, and I cast them in the lake of fire in the mighty name of Jesus! In the name of Jesus, I pray that you remove any unforgiveness I may be harboring for MYSELF. You said when I am at my weakest, you will be at your strongest. And he said unto me my grace is sufficient for you, for my strength is made perfect in your weakness most

A. Simmons

gladly therefore will I rather rejoice in my infirmities that the power of Christ may rest on me. In the name of Jesus, I receive your power right now. In the name of Jesus, I bind any attack that the enemy may be using to keep me from seeing the power and strength you've given me. No weapon formed against me shall prosper. The devil is a liar. Help me to remember those things that are lovely and true, and whatsoever things are pure, whatsoever things are just, whatsoever things are of good report If there be any virtue and if there be any praise think on these things. In the name of Jesus Christ, I pray to think on these things concerning your plans for my life. My faith and my hope has escaped me father. In the name of Jesus Christ, I command that anything that Satan has stolen from me, my faith, my hope my peace, my love, my innocence that was taken away from me as a child all be restored right now in the mighty name of Jesus. Great is your mercy towards me father.

You said that whatsoever ye shall ask in my name, that I will do it that the Father may be glorified in the Son. If ye shall ask anything in my name, you will do it." John 14: 13-14 Lord, I ask in the name

of Jesus that I be loosed right now from this abuse right now Lord.

That the chains be broken over my life and any generational curses

be removed in the name of Jesus. That you will teach me how to

follow you and keep your commandments. My life is not my own.

Lord, I know the weapons of warfare are not carnal, but mighty

through the pulling down of strongholds. The casting down of

imagination and every high thing that exalted itself against the

knowledge of God and bring into captivity every thought to the

obedience of Christ. Again, Father in the name of Jesus I pray that

every stronghold that has been placed against me by Satan be loosed

and your plan and purpose for my life be restored sevenfold in the

mighty name of Jesus.

I ask that you forgive me God for being disobedient. For giving

myself to a man that was not my husband. For all the wrong I've

done in my lifetime I ask for you forgiveness, Father. I leave anybody

that has ever hurt me in my past here at the altar today: the sexual

abuse I suffered as a child, the things I was exposed to as child, the

A. Simmons

people who disappointment me, the hurt I still deal with from my father's death and any unforgiveness in my heart I leave here today. I forgive them all Father, even Luke. I'm choosing to press towards the higher make and calling that you have for my life.

I thank you, Father, for hearing my prayer. I thank you for loving me even when I don't love myself. I thank you Lord for allowing me to call you friend in a time such as this when I feel lost, broken, and confused. Lead me and guide me out of this darkness into the marvelous light. In the mighty name of Jesus. Amen.

Chapter Twenty-Three

Ruby laid by the altar and cried for another 15 minutes. She let out every inch of hurt inside of her that night. She felt renewed and empowered in that moment like never before. She got up and quietly slipped out of the church and headed home. She checked her phone to see if Luke had called. She had one missed message from him that read, "Don't worry about picking me up. I have a ride home." So Ruby headed home and got in bed as soon as she got there. Luke got home later while Ruby was asleep.

Day 7- It was Saturday and the last day of Ruby's fast. Ruby got up about 5:30am and couldn't go back to sleep. She decided to try to find another prayer service to attend that day. She went downstairs and boiled her usual cup of morning tea and started to search for a Saturday morning prayer service. This time she found one a little further out that started at 7:30. It wasn't even 6 o'clock yet so she had plenty of time to get there. She rushed upstairs to get dressed. Luke was still sleeping. She gently tapped him on the shoulder.

"Good morning Luke, I'm headed out to a prayer service," she said.

Luke looked up at her disgusted "Yeah, whatever," he said. "God going to punish you for using him as an excuse to be a slut," he said.

Ruby shook her head laughing, "I'll pray for you while I'm there, Luke," she said walking out of the bedroom towards the stairs.

"Oh, it's funny? Don't pray for me, I'm straight. I don't need you casting none of your evil spells on me," he replied. Ruby ignored him and continued down the stairs to leave. She poured her tea in a to-go mug and headed out the door.

She got lost several times trying to find the church, but finally found it. This was a newer church separated into two buildings. On one side was the traditional church look, brown bricks with double glass doors. The other side however looked more like a one-story office building. The layout was kind of confusing, so Ruby looked for other cars and parked there. She got out and headed towards what appeared to be the entrance but to her surprise, the door was locked. She tried about three more doors before feeling like it wasn't meant for her to be there that morning. She stumbled across one more door which was in the very back of the building and it was open. "Thank God," she said. She went in and walked down a long hallway until she saw a head pop out from behind a door.

"Good morning! Are you here for prayer service?" the lady asked.

"Yes, ma'am. I am," replied Ruby. "Am I too late?" she asked.

Ruby had gotten so turned around that it was now 7:45.

A. Simmons

"No ma'am. We're just getting started. Come on in and find you a spot to pray," she said.

"Thank you," replied Ruby.

She went inside and found a seat and started to pray. The sanctuary was much smaller than the previous church and only had two columns of pews and a small pulpit. There were four other people there. Ruby didn't introduce herself to anyone she just prayed. They had gospel music playing. They all prayed for about 30 minutes until a male member of the church walked up to the microphone and began to pray for them all. When he finished, Ruby got up and gathered her things to leave.

"Thank you for coming," said the lady who had escorted her in. "What is your name?" she asked.

"Ruby Smith," replied Ruby.

"Well Ruby, we're glad you joined us this morning. Please come back anytime," she said.

"Thank you. I will," replied Ruby.

Ruby turned to walk out of the church and was stopped by a deep voice.

"Excuse me ma'am. There is something I need to tell you," he said.

Ruby turned and looked. It was the man who was praying.

"Oh Lord. What is he about to say," Ruby said to herself.

He was a tall African American male about 6'5" and weighed at least 250 pounds.

"God wanted me to tell you He forgives," he said.

Ruby's eyes got very wide as she'd just asked God for forgiveness the night before. She burst into tears.

"He also wanted me to tell you that there is somebody blocking him from you and you have to let HIM go. He is not good for you and will eventually kill you."

Ruby's heart was so full. She was crying uncontrollably. She managed to get herself together and looked the man in his eye.

A. Simmons

"You just don't know the confirmation you just gave me. Thank you," she said.

"No, I don't, but God does," he said. "Don't thank me, thank God. Now you go and be blessed and remember what God has said."

Ruby left there still in tears. She couldn't get over the fact that God had answered so directly and clearly. Now all she had to do was leave Luke and this time she was ready.

Chapter Twenty-Four

From that day on, it took Ruby three days to leave but it wasn't easy. Luke had been mean since the 6th day of her fast. She didn't know how she was going to get him out, but she knew she had to be careful because he could kill her in the process, so she waited for the right time.

Ruby had just gotten home from picking her son up from school. Luke was already at the house and drinking when they arrived. They walked in and went straight upstairs to Henry's room. Henry had been staying with his grandma for the past week until Ruby got rid of Luke, but today Ruby had to pick him up.

Ruby left Henry in the room while she went downstairs and prepared dinner. Luke didn't say a word to her. He was sitting on the sofa playing on his phone. Ruby tried not to make eye contact as much as possible.

Luke got up and headed towards the kitchen.

A. Simmons

"I'm headed to the store," said Luke.

"Okay, do you mind grabbing some juice for Henry?" she asked.

"Hell no! You can go get it yourself," he replied.

He walked back over to the sofa and sat down. "As a matter of fact, I'm about to go somewhere my ride is on the way," he said. Luke grabbed his phone and went outside.

Ruby could hear him on the phone talking.

"Man, this hoe must think I'm crazy. She can go get her own son something to drink. He's a little punk anyway. She is running around here cheating on me like it's cool. I'm going to treat her like shit," he said.

Of course, Ruby wasn't cheating on Luke but that was the lie he created in his head. He was talking so loudly that Henry could hear him upstairs.

"Mommy, what is Luke yelling for. He's scaring me. Are you okay?" Henry had come down the stairs into the kitchen with her.

"Baby I'm not sure but everything is going to be okay." She gave Henry a big hug. "You want to help me cook?" she asked.

"Yes, I will," said Henry.

Ruby had to think fast because she knew things would only escalate from there, so Ruby locked the door while Luke was outside and would not let him back in.

Luke started banging on the door.

"Let me in you evil bitch. My book bag is in there," he said.

"No, you'll have to call the police to get back in. I'm not opening this door without them."

Ruby took Henry upstairs. Luke beat on the door and rang the doorbell for the next hour. But Ruby didn't respond. She had to unplug the door bell and raise the volume on Henry's TV so he couldn't hear. Henry finally dozed off. Ruby didn't care how long Luke knocked, but she was not letting him back in unless he called the police. Finally, the knocks stopped. Ruby peeked out of the window and saw Luke trying to destroy her vehicle. She quickly grabbed her phone and started to record. Luke kicked in her back window and was trying to destroy the inside of her car. She was about to call the police and remembered what Luke had said, "If you call the police, I'll kill you before they get here." Despite Ruby being scared, she went ahead and called the police. By the time they arrived. Luke was gone.

"Do you think he's going to return to the premises?" the office asked.

"I'm not sure. I set his bookbag outside the door hoping that would make him leave." replied Ruby.

"My advice to you is to ditch this guy and never look back. You already have a protection order so if he comes back you can just call us. In my experience guys like this don't change, they get worse. We just had a lady get killed last week. Stay safe, Mrs. Smith. You can pick your police report up in 2 days and have a warrant placed for his arrest."

"Thank you, officer," she replied.

Ruby let the officer out and closed the door. That was the last day Ruby Smith allowed Luke Johnson to come near her. At least that's what she thought.

Help, I'm being Stalked!

Chapter Twenty-Five

Many years ago, I lived alone with my now 15-year-old son. We stayed in a 2-bedroom apartment in a nice upper-class neighborhood. I never had an issue with safety other than the regular precaution of being a single woman living alone with a child. One day I came home from work and my patio door was open. I thought this was strange as I always made sure everything was locked - especially my patio door. I quickly checked the apartment to see if someone was there, but the coast was clear. I started to second guess and convinced myself that I'd left it open even though I knew I didn't.

About a week past and I was on my way to drop my son off at his grandma's. We stayed about 15 miles away. I took my usual route and jumped on the freeway. About halfway there I noticed a 1990 Mercedes-Benz 560 in my rear-view mirror. It was a beauty. I didn't think much of it other than it being a nice car. Ironically, it gets off on the same exit I did. I ignored

A. Simmons

it and just assumed we were both going in the same direction.
As I got ready to make the turn to my baby's grandparents' house I was curious to see if they would make the same turn. He kept straight as I turned, so I brushed it off. I did however get a better look at the driver. It was white male in his mid to late 40's.

I dropped my son off safely and headed back home. It wasn't until I was getting off the exit to my house when I realized the same car was behind me again. "Oh my God," I said to myself. "I think I'm being followed."

I tried not to panic too much, but this was a first for me. I quickly pulled into a gas station off the exit to see what he would do. The car pulled across the street in a vacant lot. Still in denial I decided to pretend like I was going home but make turns that I normally don't. The car was right behind. I was indeed panicking then. I had to think fast so I had him follow me to the police station which was at least 10 miles away.

When he realized where we'd pulled up at, he sped off. I jumped out of the car and ran in to file a report. I was scared and for the first time in my life, I'd been stalked.

Approximately 1 in 4 women and 1 and 18 men in the United States are victims of stalking. According to the dictionary, the definition for stalking is hunting for prey, or physically following someone, or contacting them excessively. The legal definition according to the Marriam-Webster New World Law Dictionary, "stalking is a form of harassment generally comprised of repeated persistent following with no legitimate reason and with intention of harming, or so as to arouse anxiety or fear of harm in the person being followed. Stalking may also take the form of harassing telephone calls, computer communications, letter-writing etc." (https://www.merriam-webster.com/legal/stalking)

Another form of stalking that is becoming more and more common is cyberstalking. According to YourDictionary.com, cyberstalking is "sending multiple emails, often on systematic

basis to

annoy embarrass, intimidate, or threaten a person to make the

person fearful that she or a member of her family or

household will be harmed." This is also called email

harassment. Unfortunately, Ruby experienced both.

Chapter Twenty-Six

"U have no clue who u played. U will pay. The last one that played me paid. I tried my best to kill her. Her family knew I was going to get her, so they moved her out of town. Good thing about you is you think you fly. That's why I'm going to blow your brains all over the ground, but you will beg for your life first. Satan worker u dead B… You turned your back on me. You want do nobody else how you did me. I will wait until you think this shit is over and slaughter you're A… I swear to it," Sent Via Facebook by Luke.

This was one of many messages Luke sent to Ruby. One minute he wanted to kill her, next minute he was sorry and confessing his love. "I know you probably wasn't home last night to hear the scripture. I called that number you gave me, and they talked a lot about going through hard times. I felt like it was talking directly to me! I been praying to God every night to bring u back into my life! I know you probably feel like dating other people, but we belong together. I have never been so in love with a woman like I am with you. Just your voice calms me. I want to believe that we are meant to be together. Ruby, with God we can make it, I just know it. I love you so much. I can't eat or sleep." Sent Via Facebook by Luke.

Ruby had blocked Luke phone calls. It had been a couple of weeks since they'd separated, and this was the strongest she'd ever been. She did not respond - period. She decided to stay in the condo for the safety of her parents and Henry. However, it didn't matter whether Ruby was there or not Luke was still passing by. Things had gotten so bad that Ruby had to send her son to his father's house for a while. She also had to alert the principal at his school about how dangerous Luke was and Henry was not to go with him if he showed up. Even though leaving Luke was the best decision she had made, things seem to be getting worse.

Ruby was at home praying when she got a phone call from her step-dad Willie.

"Ruby, where are you?" he asked. "You need to call the police. Luke just drove by and threw all your clothes in the yard and they seem to be all cut up. This man is crazy! You better tell the police to take care of this Ruby before I have to," he said.

"Oh my God, why would he do that. Just go back inside dad. I'm calling the police." Ruby called the police and filed a police report. This went on for weeks, but Ruby was determined not to go back. She decided that she would speak out to raise awareness about domestic violence, so she reached out to a local tv station she had worked with in the past. She was ready to share her story and they were ready and willing to listen. For Ruby she felt this would not only help in the healing process but would save somebody else's life. However, the fact the Ruby spoke out made Luke more furious and what already seemed like a nightmare to Ruby was starting to feel like death.

A. Simmons

"So, Ruby tell us about your situation," the reporter asked. Ruby explained everything the best she could without ever saying Luke's name.

"I'm sure people are wondering how someone like you, a professional model and actress, could allow this to happen to her. What would you say to that question?" she asked.

"Well, I've lived such a fast-paced life that I wanted a normal relationship. I wanted to be with someone who wasn't in the industry I knew," replied Ruby.

"I've always said I'd never let a man put his hands on me. I have two brother's, military at that, who taught me how to protect myself. However, what I learned was that, you never know what you're going to do until it actually happens to you," she said.

The interview lasted about 30 minutes. Ruby left the station that night feeling free. She was finally beginning to love herself again. On the ride home, she called her friend Kimberly.

"I did it friend," Ruby said. "I'm finally feel free. I haven't felt this way in a long time. I forgot what it felt like to love me," she said.

"I am so proud of you Ruby," said Kimberly. "I heard the entire interview. You did an awesome job!" she said.

"Thanks friend. I'm going to go home and try to get some rest. I'll call you in the morning," said Ruby.

"Okay. Love you friend. If Luke shows up call the police," said Kimberly.

"I will. I'm not worried about Luke. God's got me," she replied. Ruby hung up the phone and begin to cry. She started to sing "I'm Moving Forward," by Israel Houghton and New Breed. "I'm not going back, I'm moving ahead, I'm here to declare in you, my past is over in you. All things made new. Surrender my life to Christ, I'm moving, moving forward," sang Ruby. She began to pray,

A. Simmons

"Lord I am so grateful that you have delivered me. I am so grateful for your grace and mercy. I will forever praise you because I am fearfully and wonderfully made. Though my enemy is upon me Father I will not move to a place of defeat. No weapon formed against me shall prosper. I pray for the strength of Moses right now that through this time I won't turn back despite the adversity that may lay ahead. I will not be like the Israelites and lose my faith. Thank you for delivering me out of the darkness into the marvelous light. My soul says yes to Your will and yes to Your way. Thank you for this peace that you have given me in the midst of the storm. I am in the safety of your arms so whom shall I fear? In Jesus name I pray Amen."

Chapter Twenty-Seven

It was early Monday morning. The day after Ruby's interview. Ruby woke up to her phone ringing and several missed messages from her friends, and one from the producers of the show. She was a bit relieved that the calls were not from Luke. Ruby called the producer back first.

"Hey Samantha, its Ruby returning your call. How are you?" asked Ruby.

"I'm fine," replied Samantha. "Thanks for asking. I was calling because we got a message from someone saying we need to check our sources concerning your interview yesterday. They were basically insinuating that you are lying," she said.

"Wow," replied Ruby. "I'm sure it's Luke," she said.

"Well we're going to check into it. One of our staff members will be reaching out to him," said Samantha. "I just wanted to give you a heads up that we would be getting his side of the story as well," she said.

"Thanks for the update, Samantha," replied Ruby. Ruby

didn't exactly now how to feel at this point. Needless to say,

Luke was behind it and began to paint a totally different story

to the producers and everyone else. He claimed that Ruby was

upset and was only saying these things because he cheated on

her. Ruby knew this wasn't the truth and thought nobody was

going to believe him, but she was in for a rude awakening.

Ruby immediately called Kim first. "Kim, you'll never believe

what has happened," said Ruby. Before Ruby could tell

Kimberly anything, she interrupted her.

"Ruby I have something to tell you and I don't want you to

panic," she said.

"Okay, I'm trying not to, but this doesn't sound good," said

Ruby.

"Have you been on Facebook this morning," she asked.

"No, I haven't. Kimberly tell me what's wrong," said Ruby.

"Just come over here before you log on and we can talk about it," said Kimberly.

"I'm about to log on," said Ruby.

"Wait!" said Kimberly. "Before you do just listen. Luke has started a fake Facebook page in your name. You need to know that he has posted naked pictures of you," said Kimberly.

Ruby's heart fell to the floor.

"Oh my God! Oh my God!" yelled Ruby. "No weapon formed against me shall prosper, no weapon formed against me shall prosper," Ruby said over and over again. "Lord why me, why me?" she said. "Calm down, Ruby. I'm on my way to you," Kimberly said.

Ruby sat down and logged onto Facebook and there it was, a fake Facebook page in her name.

"I am a liar! I was never a victim in a domestic violence relationship. I went on the tv and lied to hurt the person that left me. I didn't leave, he left me. I did it all for attention to raise money for my foundation," via Facebook post.

A. Simmons

This was followed by naked pictures of Ruby and a note in the comment section that read "I have four videos on xxno.com check them out!"

It was horrible. Ruby had over 25 messages from friends trying to warn her about the account.

One of her high school classmates wrote, "Hey somebody created a fake page in your name Ruby Smith and it's HORRIBLE! YOU NEED TO TRY TO GET IT SHUT DOWN. Just concerned why anyone would want to do that to you." Another person wrote "You know someone has a fake IG page for you right RubySmith6969." One of her church members wrote "There has been a page created with your name on it!!!! NOT GOOD AT ALL.

Perhaps the one that hurt her the most was the people she let down. A longtime college associate wrote "Hey lady so happy that you were able to make it out of that toxic relationship. Never in a million years would I have believed you would be in a situation like that. I have always thought of you to be beautiful, strong willed, and world traveler. From a distance I admired you. And to be truthful I still admire you for your strength to come forward. Thanks for your strength and your belief in God!!!!"

Despite the fact that Ruby was trying to stay strong, she could not take it anymore and broke down crying. Of course, Luke had sent her messages as well. One of them said, "U fake!!!!! U are what you are! U a piece of shit. I got videos to post whenever I want to Clown! Laugh now cry later! Fact."

Even though she knew the things Luke was saying wasn't true she couldn't help but cry out to God "WHY ME?" Ruby fell to her knees and prayed.

> *"Father I stretch my hands to thee. No other help I know. I want to remain steadfast and unmovable Father, but I feel like it just got hit by an earthquake. Literally, I feel like my foundation has been shaken. I am sick to my stomach Father.*

A. Simmons

This plot is too heavy to bear. I know you said you would bless me and make my name great father but surely you didn't mean in this way. You said you know the plans you have for my life. Plans to prosper me and not harm me, plans to give me hope and a future. I still believe that Father and even in this time when I don't understand why this is happening to me. Send me a word father. A refresher for my soul because it thirsts for you right now. In Jesus name I pray Amen."

Chapter Twenty-Eight

"I apologize if you have received any friendship requests over the past few days. I have had over 5 Fake Facebook pages created in my name so if you receive a friendship request for me IT'S NOT ME please report it and block it. I am currently being stalked and harassed by my ex because I decided to leave an abusive relationship. In effort to spread this message you may receive this more than once. Thank you for your support," said Ruby.

Ruby sent a mass message out to her Facebook friends to inform them about the events that had occurred. It had been 3 days and every day there was a different page in her name. Each time a page was created it was followed by a slew of messages from people informing her she'd been hacked. Ruby had to first report the page as fraudulent and wait until Facebook reviewed before they took it down. The more people that reported the page the faster they removed it. On average,

A. Simmons

the page stayed up for about 3 hours. For Ruby those 3 hours felt like eternity.

Ruby already had a restraining order out on Luke. He was not supposed to be contacting her directly or indirectly. She got in contact with her detective for her case she had against Luke to figure out what to do. "Hey Detective Lewis. I need to know what to do about Luke stalking me. He has created fake social media pages in my name. He is threatening to kill me and my family and passing by my home. Can you please call me, so we can talk? I'm starting to feel like it's not even worth going through the process for the pending felony strangulation charges I already have against him. This is horrible. Please call me back."

Ruby already had a court date the next month for the strangulation charges she already had against him. It was a felony charge so if found guilty, he would be facing prison time. She was also still going to court for the domestic violence assault charges from when Luke repeatedly beat her in the head. Ruby had thought about not pressing charges, but Luke wouldn't leave her alone. He was still calling and texting her. "When I stop calling you, your life will be over. Hope you're having a great time. I know you did while I was sick and depressed. U won't make it in the court house in the morning doll. All these calls with no answer only building up my rage. You're going to regret doing this. Laugh now cry later," sent via text message by Luke.

Ruby was beyond disgusted. She was angry, afraid, hurting, and started feeling like she did before she fasted. She honestly felt like giving up until she reached out to Alley Johnson. Mrs. Johnson was local attorney. Ruby was so hurt that she poured her heart out to Mrs. Johnson on the phone.

"Hey Mrs. Johnson, it's Ruby Smith. We meet a while ago on a prayer retreat," said Ruby.

"Ruby. Hi!," said Mrs. Johnson. "I know exactly who you are. How can I help you?" she asked.

"I'm currently being stalked by my ex. I'm afraid he will kill me. I recently left, and I currently have pending charges against him. I already have a restraining order as well. It seems like it's taking the courts forever to get justice. I need HELP. I'm working with Detective Lewis who is doing all she can at this point. I'm waiting for her to reach back out to me to advise how to get stalking charges," said Ruby.

"Oh my God, Ruby. I had no idea you were experiencing this," said Mrs. Johnson. "I'm going to help you," she said. From that day forth Ruby felt something she had lost in the past; Hope. Mrs. Johnson connected the dots between Ruby, the D.A.'s office and Detective Lewis. The next morning Ruby received a call from Detective Lewis.

"Mrs. Smith. It's Detective Lewis. How are you," she said?

"I'm scared and ready for this to be over," said Ruby.

"I got your message and I talked to Mrs. Johnson. It's going to be hard getting stalking charges against him, but we can do it. We must prove that it's him that's contacting you. All the fake pages he created and emails he's sending we must somehow track the IP address for those. Documentation is going to be your best friend and it's the only way you'll win this case. Every time he contacts you - and I do mean every time - call the police and file a report. Make sure you have your restraining order with you. Each time he violates it, a warrant can be placed for his arrest. I'll be working on getting all the social media sites subpoenaed as well as IP addresses for the emails. Again, document everything. I'll need for you to bring me copies of everything you have especially threatening messages, so we can try to get the charge filed. Do me a favor and go through every message and highlight information that only you and him would know. This will help us prove that

A. Simmons

it's him. If you need me for anything please do not hesitate to call," she said. "Thank you, Detective Lewis. I'll get the paperwork to you tomorrow," said Ruby. Ruby felt better after talking to Detective Lewis. She followed her instruction to the T. Over the course of the next 2 months, Ruby had a total of 22 police reports.

Chapter Twenty-Nine

"Good morning sister. How are you doing?" the pleasant voice said on the other end. It was Tonya calling to give Ruby some words of encouragement. "I'm doing well sister. I'm just so tired of this process. Luke is trying to do everything in his power to destroy me. We have been to several court dates and he's been told over and over again to leave me alone, but he won't. I'm extremely frustrated with the judicial system at this point because every time we go to court, the date keeps getting pushed back. Meanwhile Luke is still STALKING ME!! Instead of them going ahead and locking him up, they just keep adding things to the restraining order. Listen to these messages he's sending me sister," said Ruby.

"Yea I'm still calling you because I'm hurt. I could have another woman if I wanted to but I still want you. I'm going to wait until this is over. Laugh now cry later," sent via text message. "Ain't no hope for you. I'm risking a lot trying to

A. Simmons

talk to you. You're a piece of trash. I'm going to make sure God curses you." sent via text message. "Can't even answer and let me talk to you devil ass hoe. But I'm going to send you back to the hell you came from. You are watching me hurt but not for long though I swear to that," sent via text message. "Please just answer the phone. I need to talk to you. U don't have to talk just listen. Why are you watching me hurt? I won't sleep until I kill myself but I'm going to see you before I go. You are the worst woman I've ever met," sent via text message.

"I'm still up! Still waiting. My pain and your fun end today. I swear to that on my Father. Laugh now, your family will cry tomorrow. "all sent via text message.

Ruby continued, "He is even sending messages to my foundation website sister. One minute he wants to kill me, the next minute he still loves me." said Ruby. "Listen to this one:"

"I'm staying back at the shop. I've been so stressed just need to be alone. If you ever need me I'm here. You are the love of my life. My soulmate. These months have showed me that. I love you and I miss you. I was thinking we could put this past us and still be together. I guess my love for you is that strong. Again, I'm so sorry for my wrongs. I shouldn't have done those things to you. I love you and miss you so much. Take care beautiful," sent via email.

"Sister you're not falling for any of this are you?" asked Tonya.

"Absolutely not. I know now there is no way that Luke can love me. However, I do believe he will try to kill me. Something is wrong with him. I keep praying for God to fix it sister and honestly, I'm even starting to get frustrated with God because he hasn't yet," replied Ruby.

"Think about it this way. You just told me you have no desire of being with Luke again, so God has definitely delivered you from that stronghold! I remember when you would call my phone crying because you couldn't let him go. Trust me sister God will deliver you from Luke's evil threats and you shall LIVE and not DIE," said Tonya. "I want you to remember this scripture:

> "*Fret not thyself because of evildoers, neither be thou envious against the workers of iniquity. For they shall soon be cut down like the grass, and wither as the green herb. Trust in the LORD and do good so shalt thou dwell in the land, and verily thou shalt be fed. Delight thyself also in the LORD; and he shall give thee the desires of thine heart. Commit thy way unto the Lord; trust also in him; and he shall bring it to pass. And he shall bring forth thy righteousness as the light, and thy judgment as the noonday. Rest in the LORD, and wait patiently for him: fret not thyself because of him who prosperity in his way, because of the man who bringeth wicked devices to pass. Cease from anger and forsake wrath: fret not thyself in any ways to do evil. For the evildoers shall be cut off: but those that wait upon the Lord, they shall*

inherit the earth. For yet a little while, and the wicked shall

not be; yea, thou shalt diligently consider his place, and it

shall not be," Psalms 37: 1-10.

"Trust me sister he may think he's winning, but God won't

allow this to happen much longer. One thing about God, he

will do what he said he would do," said Tonya.

"Thank you, sister, I needed that. I'm going to print it out and

read it every day. I was praying that God would send me a

word to find comfort in peace and he just did!!!" said Ruby. "I

have to move in the next couple of weeks because it's not safe

here anymore. Luke is still passing by," said Ruby.

"Good. Well I'd plan on surprising you and coming to see you

two weeks from today. Just let me know what I need to do,"

said Tonya.

"Thank you, sister. I will. Love you," said Ruby.

"Love you too," replied Tonya.

Ruby hung up the phone and got ready to head out to see her

detective. They had a meeting with the District Attorney's

office that day to try an obtain a felony stalking charge on Luke. She prayed before leaving out the door.

> *"Lord thank you for sending me a word today. Thank you for delivering me Lord. Continue to send your angels out to protect me. I will fret not Father for soon Luke's evilness will be cut off in the mighty name of Jesus. Go before me and Detective Lewis today that the District Attorney will have no choice but to grant the charges. Let your name be exalted in our conversation today. In the name of Jesus. Amen"*

Chapter Thirty

Ruby arrived at the court house at 10:00am. She wore a long black skirt with a white and black shirt form her foundation and cute comfy sandals. Her hair was braided and pulled upped. Parking was always crazy at the court house, so she had to circle a few times. Everything about this place was eerie for Ruby.

The court house was a 9-story building with a water fountain in the front with a couple of status. Connected to the courthouse was the county jail which had to be at least 15 stories high. The windows on the building were small rectangle shaped and appeared at the top of the room instead of in the middle. For a brief moment Ruby visualized Luke standing up in the chair trying to glance out of the window of his jail cell. She begins to think of how miserable it would be. She couldn't imagine being trapped inside a small room with only a small pocket of light from the outside. In that moment she begins to feel sorry for Luke and thought about just leaving all the court stuff alone, but she was quickly reminded

why she had to when her phoned dinged. It was yet another

message from Luke that said, "Laugh now cry later." Ruby

immediately snapped out of it and walked in the court house.

The entrance of the court house was surrounded by

glass with big glass double doors. Ruby walked in and took a

moment to observe her surroundings. She'd only been there

one other time for court. To the left was a big TV monitor with

images of wanted criminals. To the front of her was what

seemed like a mile long roped off line followed by a metal

detector and security. She could she Detective Lewis waving

and waiting at the other end in an all-black suit. She was an

African American female, about 5'8, and tough.

"Good Morning Ruby. Are you ready," she asked.

"Good Morning Detective Lewis.

"I'm a little nervous but I'm ready. He actually just threatened

me through text so I'm more than ready," replied Ruby.

"Do you have all your paperwork?" she asked.

"Yes ma'am," replied Ruby.

"Great. Just be calm. We're going to walk in and present all the evidence we have and see what the DA says," said Detective Lewis "I'm going to be honest," she continued, "Obtaining a stalking warrant is extremely difficult, and they could very well say no."

"I understand," replied Ruby. They walked about ¼ mile down the hall way and entered the double doors to the DA's office.

Chapter Thirty-One

The office was sleek and quiet. Unlike the prison next door, it had floor-to-ceiling windows. There were 3 sofas, a chair, and two coffee tables with magazines to browse through while you wait. To the left was another set of tall glass doors that led to each DA's private office. To the right was a small private conference room followed by a long L shaped receptionist desk with a beautiful mirror behind it. "Can I help you?" said the voice behind the desk. It was a petite older African American female with snow white hair.

"Yes," replied Detective Lewis. "We are here to see Mrs. Dawson," she said.

"Is she expecting you?" the receptionist asked.

"Yes, ma'am she is. Let her know it's Detective Lewis," she replied. The receptionist picked up the phone and buzzed Mrs. Dawson. "You have a Detective Lewis and what's your name ma'am?" the receptionist asked looking over her square glasses with pointed edges.

"Ruby Smith," replied Ruby.

"And a Ruby Smith," she continued.

"Send them in," said Mrs. Dawson.

"Will do," the receptionist replied. She hung up the phone and sent them through the glass double doors to Mrs. Dawson office.

Ruby followed behind Detective Lewis. Under her breath, she was saying the Lord's Prayer: "Our Father which art in heaven, hallowed be thy name, thy kingdom come, thy will be done on earth as it is in heaven. Give us this day our daily bread and forgive us our debts as we forgive our debtors and lead me not into temptation but deliver me from evil." Ruby was interrupted by a loud voice and big smile.

"Good morning, ladies," said Mrs. Dawson standing outside her door. She'd walked out to greet them. She was an extremely tall Caucasian woman with a short haircut. She

A. Simmons

looked so much like the nationally known pastor Joyce Myers that Ruby was tempted to ask if they were related.

"Good Morning," said Detective Lewis with a hand shake.

"Good Morning," said Ruby with a hand shake as well.

"Come in and have a seat," said Mrs. Dawson.

The office was fairly small but warm and welcoming. Behind her desk there was a small table waterfall. The chairs were brown and comfortable. You could tell she was big on family as she had pictures of her husband, kids, and grandchildren on her desk and wall. Ruby studied all the pictures trying to see if Joyce Myers was in one, but she wasn't. Ruby did notice that Mrs. Dawson had several awards that she'd earned over the course of her career. She was confident that she was speaking to the right person at this point.

"You have a beautiful family," said Ruby.

"Thank you," replied Mrs. Dawson. "They are my pride and joy," she said. "So, what brings you all here?" Mrs. Dawson asked.

"As you know we have been communicating about Mrs. Smith's case," replied Detective Lewis. "I think we may finally have enough evidence to get the stalking warrant," she said.

"Ok to be charged with Stalking in The First Degree the person must be intentionally and repeatedly following or harassing another person and making and expressed or implied threat to put that person in reasonable fear of death or serious physical harm," Mrs. Dawson replied. "As long as you can show me those things we shouldn't have a problem," she said.

Ruby straightened her body in her seat. She pulled out a brown manila folder and placed it on Mrs. Dawson's desk. "I have all that and more right here, Mrs. Dawson," said Ruby. "Luke has repeatedly and is currently stalking me through email, social media, text, phone, and following me. He has also threatened to kill me and my family. We were able to match the IP address from his personal email address with the fake email accounts he created," she said. Ruby laid all the paperwork out on Mrs. Dawson's desk.

"Wow you were actually able to match the IP addresses," Mrs. Dawson asked. "Yes, ma'am," replied Ruby. She pointed to the highlighted area on both his address and the one on the fake email.

"Yep they match." said Mrs. Dawson. "Detective Lewis your team has verified this information correct?"

"Yes, ma'am they did," replied Detective Lewis.

"I was also able to trace back the numbers from the blocked messages. I had to download an app called TrapCall to my phone to do it, but it works. TrapCall reveals the phone number for the blocked number that's trying to contact you. I printed out a copy of my missed call log showing the blocked numbers and paired it with the call log from TrapCall to reveal the number. I also printed a copy of my phone bill. You can see that the same number he used to contact me with his name is the exact number he used to threaten and harass me through text message. Also, you can see on the phone log some days he called over 100 times within 1 hr.," Ruby explained. "Here is one where he threatens to kill me," Ruby handed the paper to Mrs. Dawson.

"You turned your back on me. You want do nobody else how you did me. I will wait until you think this shit is over and slaughter your ass swear to it, "Mrs. Dawson said reading the text message out loud. "This guy is really sick," she said. "I also have copies of over 22 police reports for the past 2 months. If you turn to the next page..."

"I don't need to hear anymore, Mrs. Smith. The evidence is sufficient. You have done what most victims fail to do and that is document everything. I am granting the warrant for

A. Simmons

Felony Stalking in first degree. You'll need to take the paper down to the judge for bail amount. The maximum bail is $150,000 and I strongly suggest it be set for that amount, however the judge will need to make that call. Good luck, Mrs. Smith. Be sure to keep documenting everything and stay safe," she said.

Ruby began to cry. "Thank you so much, Mrs. Dawson," she said. Both Detective Lewis and Ruby left the office and headed down to see the judge. They got on the elevators and Ruby broke down in tears. "Thank you, God," Ruby said out loud. She looked over at Detective Lewis and she was crying as well.

"Today is proof that prayer works and God is real," she said. "Your faith is unbelievable Mrs. Smith," she continued. "Out of my 10 years of being a detective, this the first Felony Stalking Warrant I've been able to get. You did an excellent job of documenting everything. Now let's see what this judge has to say."

The elevator stopped and they both got off. Detective Lewis walked over to the judge and spoke with him private. Ruby stood in the back. It took about 5 minutes before Detective Lewis turned around with a smile. "The warrant has been filled and his bail has been set for $150,000," Detective Lewis said excitedly.

"Are you serious. Thank you, Lord. This is almost over!" Ruby said.

"We still have to go to court so make sure you keep documenting everything," she said.

"Thank you, Detective Lewis," said Ruby.

Ruby left the courtroom full of joy and excitement. She got to her car and burst into tears praising and thanking God. She began to pray,

"Father, thank you. Thank you, Father. You deserve all the glory and the honor and the praise. Thank you for answering

my prayers. Thank you making what seemed to be impossible, possible. Continue to order my footsteps, Father. Help me that I may put on the breastplate of righteousness and the shield as I continue to walk through this battle. Father, I know you said the battle is not mine but yours Father and I am holding on to your hand. Lead me and guide me so that I will not go astray. Thank you for the support system you've given me. You didn't have to do it, but you did today and every day. Hallelujah is the highest praise. Continue to make my enemy my footstool. Thank you for making me the head and not the tail. Above and not beneath. Mostly thank you for loving me unconditionally. In Jesus name I pray. Amen."

Finding Closure

A. Simmons

Chapter Thirty-Two

"Better is the end of a thing than the beginning thereof and the patient in spirit is better than the proud in spirit." Ecclesiastes 7:8

Closure. What is it? How hard is it to accept it? According to vocabulary.com, closure is the end or the closing down of something. It can be physical – like the closure of your local library – or emotional, like the closure you experience when you finally come to terms with the end of a romance. Closure can take months, weeks and sometimes years but it's necessary.

I host a small group every Tuesday particularly for the underserved women in the community who've been faced with a crisis, addiction, parenting issues, and domestic violence relationships to name of few. Today it has blossomed into a group of women from all walks of life. Perhaps the most challenging issue they must deal with is closure. They need more than the air we breathe. Recently one of the ladies spoke about how to get over her ex. It had been going on eight months now and she still couldn't get him off her mind. She needed help and wanted answers. It was almost as if she needed a step by step play book of what to do. Although I think there is no "Closure Playbook" filled with rules that will work for everyone, I do believe there are steps we can incorporate when trying to find closure.

I read an interesting article by the Huffington Post titled "How to Finally Get Closure After A Split, In 9 Expert-Approved Steps." I would like to address the first 4 steps.

Step 1 is to recognize that there is no time table for moving on. In my opinion, healing takes time. It is a process that is necessary to heal and move forward. "There is no right time for closure. If you try to rush the process, you may end up short-changing yourself," said Tiffany Hammond, a life coach based in the greater Denver area.

A. Simmons

Step 2 is to give yourself permission to feel sad. Yes, it's

okay to cry. Sob if you need to. Phone a friend and just cry on

the phone. Find a shoulder to cry on or lock yourself in a room

and just LET IT OUT! Chelli Pumphrey, a counselor based in

Denver, Colorado, says it's important to cycle through all your

emotions: sadness, disappointment, guilt, total rage – but only

up to a point. The goal should be to process and release those

emotions, not dwell on them in an unhealthy way.

Step 3 in my opinion is by far the most important and

the hardest. "FORGIVE YOUR EX." If you're anything like me

at some point you feel like the person doesn't deserve to be

forgiven. It's important for us to remember that forgiveness is

not for the other person, it's for you. Alicia H. Clark, a

psychologist based in Washington, D. C. said "What's even

more difficult is forgiving yourself for your mistake. Self-

forgiveness helps you get to the bottom of why your

relationship failed and prepares you for your next

relationship." I couldn't agree more. Outside of forgiving the other person, it's equally as important to forgive yourself. I like to think of it this way, God has forgiven me for all my shortcomings, the least I could do is forgive myself and others. The last step I would like to address is step 4, accepting that you may never get an apology from your ex. Are you serious? The least he could do is apologize. It's human nature for us to feel that way. Unfortunately, this is not the case. Vikki Stark, a psychotherapist and the director of the Sedona Counseling Center of Montreal said, "Many people get stuck psychologically longing for an indication that their ex recognizes the pain they caused," she continued, "You may need to accept that your ex has moved on and will never make that acknowledgement." This is a sad reality but so true.

Again, the healing process is different when dealing with closure on any level. Whether it be grief from the death of a love one, leaving a job where your talents weren't appreciated, going through a divorce, or fleeing from an abusive lover: healing takes time. Despite the hurt, there is hope. When we look at the scripture Ecclesiastes 7:8 it starts off saying, "Better is the end of a thing then the beginning therefore," which is true when dealing with closure. In the beginning, we deal with the hurt, pain, shame, disappointment and even guilt but once we heal there's a beautiful rainbow with a pot of gold at the end.

Chapter Thirty-Three

Ruby was so excited! For the first time since she'd left Luke, she finally felt like justice was being served for her. Luke didn't stay in jail for too long before his family came to bail him out. Ruby didn't care one bit if they did - she had the charges and planned to prosecute to the fullest. Of course, Luke continued to pass by her house and threaten her and she documented everything. The police started to patrol her house at night time. The last thing she needed to do was move and now was the time. She called her brother and sister to schedule a family meeting to update them on what was going on.

"Hey sister," Ruby said to Nichole. "I wanted to see if you could meet me for dinner tonight around 7?"

"Yes ma'am. Are you going to tell me that Luke is finally in jail for good?" said Nichole.

"Not quite sister but his punishment is coming. Trust me God is going to handle Mr. Luke," she said

A. Simmons

"I know He just needs to hurry up. That's all I'm saying," Nichole says laughing. "I'll see you there at 7. Do I need to call your brother?"

"Yes please. Thank you, sister," replied Ruby. The two hung up the phone.

Ruby had a big day. She was waiting on a phone call from a mortgage company to sign the paperwork for her new home. It's not easy trying to find a safe place when you're being stalked. She'd spent the past few days staying at the Ritz Hotel with her niece Ashley and son Henry for safety. She'd tried to be as transparent as possible with the mortgage company about her current situation. Unfortunately, she'd been turned down a few times but she'd finally found a house that was secluded and safe. She hadn't told anybody just yet, but she would tonight at dinner.

The house was perfect. It was located about 10 minutes outside of town. There were only 5 other houses and it was a dead-end street. It was white with big bay windows with a rose garden in front and a silver tin roof. There were three different sets of stairs that led to small front porch with a wicker rocking chair. She had about 2 acres of beautiful land. Trees lined the front entrance of the house. It almost felt like a tropical forest if you walked beneath them as they connected with the neighbor's trees across the street. There was a creek that ran beside her half-a-mile long driveway. She had a private balcony overlooking her backyard. The house was literally surround by nature.   Her favorite part of the house was the huge cross that was painted on the entrance of the door and the crosses engraved in the ground. She'd prayed for a place where God's presence was before she arrived and once again He'd answered her prayers.

Ruby finally got the call from the mortgage company and headed over to sign the paperwork. When she arrived, she was surprised to be greeted by the previous owners of the house. "Hey Ruby, I'm Richard Johnson and this is my wife Peggy," he said. "We just wanted to meet you. We'd googled you and saw the amazing work you're doing in the Lakeside community," he said. "We are honored to be doing business with you and pray that God will continue to protect you in the horrible situation you're in."

"Thank you, Mr. and Mrs., Johnson. You don't know how much what you just said means to me," replied Ruby.

"No need to say thank you. We also want you to know that God put it on our hearts to waive the deposits and fees," he said.

"Are serious? Thank you.! Thank you," said Ruby. "You all have truly blessed me today and I am so grateful." Ruby was extremely low on cash. She'd literally drained her savings account trying to help support Luke.

"Well when you're doing the work of the Lord as you are, he will bless you in places you least expect it. All we ask is that you keep being obedient," he said.

"Oh, don't worry I will. God has delivered me into a new season in my life and there is no turning back," she said. They shook hands and Ruby signed the paperwork and walked away with her keys. She rushed home to get ready for dinner to share the exciting news with her family.

Chapter Thirty-Four

It was 6:45pm when Ruby arrived at the restaurant. She was greeted by her sister Nichole, her brother Kenneth, and her sister-in-law Winnie. She'd chosen a Japanese restaurant. The ambiance was perfect. The lights were dimmed, and soft music played. It was a Tuesday night, so the restaurant was empty. They all piled into a booth. Before Ruby could say anything, her brother Kenneth begin to speak.

"Listen I have been keeping quiet about everything that is has been going on. However, I will say this: I have a wife and two daughters that I love very much but if Luke doesn't stop soon, and I do mean soon, I'm going to have to stop him myself," he said. Kenneth was the youngest of Ruby's two brothers. She also had an older brother name Anthony; a CIA agent who lived in South Carolina. Kenneth stood about 6'5 and was a Vice President at a local bank. He was a military man, so he trained to protect his country and at this point Ruby was his country.

"I understand brother, but we are going to let God handle him. As much as I would like for something bad to happen to him I will not be revengeful," said Ruby. "I don't want any of my family getting involved. This is my mess. I put myself in it and that's not you all's fault. The last thing I need is for my family to fall apart trying to protect me. We have to let God fight this battle for us."

"Look sister I understand what you are saying but I meant what I said," replied Kenneth.

"I'm just happy you are finally over him," Winnie said.

"Me too. I'm still healing. There are still days when I think about what we could've been if he only stopped. Every day I have to choose to be free from him. It doesn't help that he's still stalking me daily, but I took a vow to God that I would NOT be afraid of him. Of course, I'm constantly looking over my shoulders and try to be in the house before dark, but I'm not running from him," said Ruby.

"Sister, we just want you to be safe," Nichole said. "There's no reason for you to be running around town hiding. You already know how I feel about Luke. I'm starting to pray for him myself because somebody is going to hurt him. You have too many people that love you," she said. "What are you doing about moving?"

"You don't want to just go back to the house with mom and Willie?" Kenneth asked. "No, I don't want to put them in danger," replied Ruby. "Sister, I'm actually glad you asked because that's our reason for meeting tonight. I found a place about 10 minutes from Lakeside. It's secluded and safe. There's no way you'd even know houses were back there unless you were told. I signed the paper work and got my keys. I've already informed the neighbors about Luke and they have pictures so If they see him the police will be called.

Everybody has dogs as well so if there is any suspicious movement I'll know it. The only thing is...I'll need your help moving brother," she said.

"Just let me know when and I'm ready," he said. "Are you sure it's safe, Ruby?"

"Yes, I'm sure. I'll be moving this Saturday and we will have police escorts just in case Luke tries to show up and follow us," Ruby said.

"Ok, I'll be there on Saturday with help. Just know that we will have protection as well," Kenneth said.

"What are the courts saying about the charges?" asked Winnie

"Right now, I'm just playing the waiting game for it to go to trial. Every time we go to court the date gets rescheduled. It's REALLY frustrating because in the meantime he can continue to stalk and harass me. All I can do is call the police and file a report. He keeps going to jail, but apparently, he doesn't seem to care. He's pretty much making a mockery out of the judicial system in my opinion. He goes to court and pretends to be Mr. Nice Guy and all he gets is a slap on the wrist until we go to trial," said Ruby. "Another thing that's really frustrating is the abuser has the right to obtain his own attorney while the victim is forced to use a state appointed attorney. I've tried to pay someone to represent me to speed up the process, but I'm not allowed to. Not only that, I've already had two different attorneys because they keep getting rotated. If it wasn't for my God I would be dead and gone because they're not doing all they can to protect the victims."

"Now that's ridiculous," said Nichole. "Well, you're right sister, God is protecting you so whom shall you fear?"

"Exactly," replied Ruby.

"Well I need to go pick up the girls, so I will see you on Saturday," said Kenneth.

"I need to be going as well," said Nichole.

"Me too. It's getting late and I need to get in. Thank you, guys, for coming tonight. I'll see you Saturday brother," said Ruby.

They all hugged and departed ways. Ruby drove as fast as she could home, constantly checking her rear-view mirror to make sure she wasn't being followed. She made it home safely and sent a group text message that read "I'm home and safe," to her brother and sister. She hoped she would make it through the night without Luke contacting her...but soon after arriving home, her phone began to ring nonstop for the next two hours.

Chapter Thirty-Five

Saturday had finally arrived, and Ruby was ready to move. Kimberly and Jolie had come over early in the week to help Ruby pack. Luke must have sensed something was going on because as soon as her brother and police arrived with the U-Haul, Luke started calling. It was as if he was hiding in the bushes and maybe he was, but he wasn't going to come out in front of the police.

"So, what do we need to move first?" her brother asked.

"Whatever works best for you. Everything is going," said Ruby.

It took about two hours to get the truck loaded. Luke called the whole time. At one-point Ruby gave her phone to the police and they answered it. Of course, he didn't say anything, but they knew it was him.

They headed out to the new location. There was a police car in front of them, followed by Ruby, then her brother in the U-Haul, and another police car behind them. They successfully made it to her new place without any site of Luke. The police had a clear description of his car.

They got everything unpacked.

"If you don't need us for anything else Mrs. Smith, we're going to be leaving," said the Officer. "Remember to be safe. If I were you I would purchase a can of wasp spray and keep it by the door. It can shoot up to 20 feet and is more accurate than mace. If you need us, call us."

"Thank you, officers," replied Ruby.

"Yeah, we're going to go ahead and get out of here, too," her brother said. "I love you, sister."

"Okay, love you too, brother," he replied.

Everybody had left. Ruby sat in the middle of the floor and cried tears of joy. She was so happy she had escaped. She knew the road was still long as they still had to go back to court, but the hardest part was over. She'd finally manage to get over Luke and was getting back to a healthy place. There was only one more thing Ruby needed to do.

A. Simmons

On Monday morning Ruby got up at her usual time. She got dressed and looked at herself in the mirror. "You can do this," she said.

Hesitantly Ruby grabbed her things and left. She drove for about 15 minutes before pulling up at an all white house with a long white porch that wrapped completely around the house. The porch was lined with white wicker rocking chairs. Ruby parked her car and walked up on the porch. She looked up towards the roof and said, "Lord, I don't want to do this, but I know it's necessary for my healing," said Ruby. She opened the door and went in. There was a fireplace to her left with a white sofa and loveseat. It felt warm and cozy. "May I help you?" Ruby looked to her right and there was a lady standing in front of a desk with a huge smile on her face. "Yes ma'am. My name is Ruby Smith. I'm a survivor of domestic violence and I think I may need counseling."

The End

Tribute To The Author
By: Jessica Harris

When life gets so hard,
And crazy all throughout.
Just drop down to your knees and,
PRAY YOUR WAY OUT!

When people put you down,
And fill you with self-doubt.
Just know that you are somebody,
and PRAY YOUR WAY OUT!

Sometimes good things flood you,
Sometimes there's a drought.
No matter what the storms may bring,
just PRAY YOUR WAY OUT!

When you want the burdens lifted,
And you're ready for a new route.
The first thing you must do is,
PRAY YOUR WAY OUT!

When Satan is attacking,
And you need to scream and shout.
Ignore all of his tricks and games,
and PRAY YOUR WAY OUT!

God is gonna change you,
And make you like a spout.
For the blessings to pour from you,
All because you PRAY YOUR WAY OUT!

References

- Every 15 seconds a woman is abused in the U.S. It does not discriminate against age, race, gender, or financial status (Uniform Crime Reports, Federal Bureau of Investigation, 1991)
- Every 1 and 3 American women will be the victim of abuse at least once in their lifetime. (Center of Disease Control and Prevention 2017)
- The Assistant Director of Human Development and Family Studies at the University of Illinois, Jennifer Hardesty found that ultimately survivors want to be physically and emotionally connected again. Pg. 45 paragraph 2 (Article from the University of Illinois by Lyndal Khaw, "For Abused Women, leaving is a Complex and Confusing Process)
- There is a 75% chance a victim will die trying to escape their abuser. Pg. 46 paragraph 1 (Domestic Abuse Shelter of the Florida Keys)
- Since 2003, over 18,000 women have been killed by domestic violence. Pg. 46 paragraph 2 (Centers for Disease Control and Prevention. "30 Shocking Domestic Violence Statistics That Remind Us It's An Epidemic by Alanna Vagianos, published on 10/23/2014 at 9:25am ET. Updated Dec. 6, 2017, Huffpost)
- A victim will go back 7-10 times before they actually leave. Pg.47 Paragraph 1 ("Abuse: More Common than you think," By Ashely Strehl, Megah Maharry, Montana McCullough, Published April 26, 2018)
- Maya Angelou's history paraphrased pg. 25-26 (Wikipedia)

- Conversation between Maya Angelou and mother pgs. 27-28 Paragraphs 1-2 "You know I think you are one of the greatest women I've ever meet," her mother said. "Mary McCleod Bethune, Eleanor Roosevelt, and my mother: you are in that category." (Dr. Maya Angelou-Love Liberates, by Lencha Sanchez, published on March 4, 2013 https://youtu.be/cbecKv2xR14)
- Casey Gwinn references to strangulation pg. 31 paragraph 3 (Blog at WordPress.com, Should The Victim Fight Back? By Kia, Jan. 2015)
- Paraphrased information on verbal abuse from Harvard University pgs. 70-71, paragraphs 3-4. (April 2007, The Harvard Gazette published an article by William J. Cormie.)
- Words of affirmation pg. 71 ("The Five Love Languages," by Gary Chapman pg. 37, Love Language #1)
- History of Rosa Parks paraphrased pgs. 88-90, paragraphs 1-4 (Published on Jan 26, 2010 by Biography https://youtu.be/v8A9gvb5Fh0)
- "There is only so much hurt, disappointment and oppression one can take. The line between reason and madness grows thinner," pg. 88 Paragraph 1 (How history got the Rosa Parks story wrong, By Jeanne Theoharis, Dec. 1, 2015 paragraph 10)
- As a young child she watched her grandfather stand guard over their family because, at any moment the KKK could come and burn down their home and them(paraphrased). Pg. 88 Paragraph 2 (How history got the Rosa Parks story wrong, By Jeanne Theoharis, Dec. 1, 2015 paragraph 14-15)

- "I had been pushed around all my life and I felt in that moment I couldn't take it anymore." Pg. 90 Paragraph 1 (The Guardian, Rosa Parks archive heads to Library of Congress: "I had been pushed around all my life" by Ed Pilkington in New York, Tue. 3 Feb. 2015 14.00 Est. paragraph 7)
- Approximately 1 in 4 women and 1 and 18 men in the United States are victims of stalking pg. 142 paragraph 1 (National Coalition Against Domestic Violence)
- Legal definition of stalking pg. 142 ((https://www.merriam-webster.com/legal/stalking)
- Legal definition for cyberstalking pg. 142 (YourDictionary.com)
- The 9 expert approved steps to finding closure paraphrased . Pgs. 180-182 Paragraphs 2-6 (How to Finally Get Closure After a Split, in 9 Expert-Approved Steps," by Brittany Wong, Published 03/21/2016 8:32pm, updated March 22, 2016. Huffpost)

"He Moves Me" is dedicated to my husband Larry Simmons

Made in United States
Orlando, FL
15 July 2022

19841458R00115